CALⱯINISM: PU_

CALVINISM: PURE AND MIXED

A Defence of the Westminster Standards

WILLIAM G. T. SHEDD, D.D.

THE BANNER OF TRUTH TRUST

THE BANNER OF TRUTH TRUST
3 Murrayfield Road, Edinburgh EH12 6El
PO Box 621, Carlisle, Pennsylvania 17013, USA

*

© *The Banner of Truth Trust 1986*
First published 1893
First Banner of Truth edition 1986
Reprinted 1999
ISBN 0 85151 7676

*

Typeset 1n 101/2/12pt Linotron Plantin
At The Spartan Press Ltd, Lymington, Hants
Printed and bound in Great Britain by
Bookcraft (Bath) Ltd.,
Midsomer Norton.

Contents

PREFACE

The object of this work is to define and defend the tenets of Calvinism in their original purity and self-consistence, as distinguished from proposed modifications of them for the purpose of an alleged improvement. It has grown out of the proposal introduced into the Northern Presbyterian Church, to revise the Westminster Standards. It contains the substance of a pamphlet which the author published in opposition to this proposal when it was first made, together with discussions of several important subjects that have subsequently come up for examination during the controversy in the Church. Of these, preterition, common and special grace, original sin, infant salvation, the 'larger hope', and the inerrancy of Scripture, are the most prominent. The controversy has disclosed the fact, that some Presbyterians deny that God may justly pass by any of mankind in the bestowment of saving grace; and assert that common grace may become saving grace by the sinner's co-operation, that original sin is not deserving of eternal death and therefore that infants are not liable to it, that the Westminster Standards teach that all the heathen are lost, and that the autographs of the inspired writers contained more or less of error. The writer endeavors to show that the first opinion is fatal to the doctrine of Divine sovereignty in election; that the second is Arminian synergism, not Calvinistic monergism; that the third destroys the doctrine of infant salvation, by making it only a quasi-salvation and a matter of obligation on the part of God; and that the fourth and fifth are mis-statements of the contents of the Confession.

When the revision of the Standards was first suggested by a few presbyteries, the great majority of the denomination had expressed no desire for it, and the measure seemed to be the scheme of only a dis-satisfied few. But it soon appeared that such dis-satisfaction with the denominational creed was considerably widespread. The presbyteries voted to revise their creed by a decisive majority. This majority soon showed itself to be composed of a conservative and radical wing. The former have endeavored to revise in conformity with the vote of the General Assembly, that no changes shall be made that impair the integrity of the Calvinistic system. The latter have proposed alterations, relating principally to the doctrines of election and preterition, which, the writer endeavors to prove, seriously impair it.

The history of the revision movement, thus far, confirms the author in his opinion, expressed at the very first, that the revision of a creed is *latitudinarian* in its nature and influence. The proposal to revise a creed is commonly made, not for the purpose of preserving its strictness, and still less to make it stricter, but in order to make it looser or more 'liberal', as the phrase is. This explains the fact, that there has never been a revision of any of the great creeds of Christendom. When latitudinarian parties have arisen in the Church, and have attempted to change the received symbols, the result has been that new creeds were formed for the new parties, and the old remained unaltered. The Semi-Arians and Arians could not induce the Ancient Church to revise the Apostles', Nicene, and Constantinopolitan creeds, in accordance with their views of an improved Trinitarianism. The Middle Ages witnessed no attempts to revise the great œcumenical symbols. None of the creeds of the Reformation, Lutheran or Calvinistic, have been revised. The only examples that border on revision are the Augsburg Variata and the Formula Concordiæ. The first was only the individual work of Melanchthon, who wished to introduce synergism into the Lutheran monergism, and not that of a church demanding it; and the last claimed to be, and actually was, a closely reasoned and logical development of the Augsburg Confession – the only instance that we recall in which revision resulted in a stricter orthodoxy. The reduction of the Forty-two Articles of Edward the Sixth to the Thirty-nine Articles of Elizabeth, cannot be called a revision. The attempt of the Remonstrants to Arminianize the Heidelberg and Belgic Confessions was a failure, and resulted in the Five Articles of the new creed.

These facts go to show that revision, speaking generally, means the alteration of doctrinal statements by injecting into them more or less of foreign elements not properly belonging to them, in order to meet a change of views in a larger or smaller part of the denomination. By this method, Calvinism, or Arminianism, or Socinianism, or any creed whatever, becomes mixed instead of pure; a combination of dissimilar materials, instead of a simple uncompounded unity. This is the destruction of that self-consistence which is the necessary constituent of true science, and indispensable to permanent power and influence. The purest and most unmixed Socinianism, Arminianism, Lutheranism, or Calvinism, is the strongest in the long run.

While the author contends that such is the nature and tendency of creed-revision, he believes that many of those who are advocating a revision of the Westminster Standards have no desire to weaken their statements or their influence. The distinction between doctrines and persons, projects and their advocates, is a valid one. One may have no confidence in a doctrine or project, and yet may have confidence in a particular advocate of it, because a person may be different in his spirit and intention from the nature and tendency of his doctrine or project, while this is a fixed quantity. Coleridge, in a conversation with a Unitarian friend, said: 'I make the greatest difference between *ans* and *isms*. I should deal insincerely with you, if I said that I thought Unitarianism is Christianity; but God forbid that I should doubt that you and many other Unitarians are in a practical sense very good Christians.' ('Table Talk,' April 4, 1832.) When the opponent of revision asserts that revision is anti-Calvinistic in its logic and tendency, he does not assert that all of its advocates are anti-Calvinists. The writer believes that the natural effect of the proposed changes in the Confession, especially those of the radical wing, will be to weaken and break down the Calvinistic system contained in it, and endeavors to prove it; but he does not believe or say that this is the desire and intention of all who urge them.

The spirit of revision, it is said, is 'in the air', and this is assigned as a reason why it should be stimulated and strengthened. This would also be a reason for the increase of malaria. It is undoubtedly true that the desire to revise the Calvinistic creed is pervading Pan-Presbyterianism to a degree not imagined at first. If it continues to increase, there can be little doubt that the historical Calvinism will be considerably modified; and doctrinal modification is an inclined plane. In an age of materialism in philosophy, and universalism in religion, when the Calvinistic type of doctrine is more violently opposed than any other of the evangelical creeds, because of its firm and uncompromising nature, the Presbyterian Church should not revise the creed from which it has derived its past solidarity and power, but should *reaffirm* it; and non-revision is reaffirmation.

The aim of the author is twofold: first, to explain some of the more difficult points in Calvinism, and thereby promote the reaffirmation of the Westminster Standards pure and simple, precisely as they were adopted by both schools in the reunion of 1870, instead of the revision of them as now proposed, which had it been urged at that time would have been fatal to the cause of reunion; and secondly, to justify and defend before the human understanding, that intellectual and powerful system of theology which had its origin in the Biblical studies and personal experience of the two most comprehensive and scientific theologians of Christendom, Aurelius Augustine and John Calvin.

NEW YORK, February 1893.

PUBLISHER'S INTRODUCTION

This book comes from a generally forgotten controversy at the end of the last century over proposals to revise the Westminster Confession of Faith in the Presbyterian Church in the United States of America. In 1889 the General Assembly of that denomination was overtured by a number of presbyteries seeking credal revision. In the opinion of Philip Schaff, that Assembly 'opened a new chapter in the history of American theology', and he expressed the belief that 'The old Calvinism is fast dying out'. A Committee on Revision was appointed and when its Final Report was issued it confirmed that it was indeed the Calvinism of the Confession which was the chief concern of those wanting revision. An amendment of the doctrinal content of the Confession required the support of two-thirds of the Church's presbyteries and when the General Assembly of 1893 met it was found that, while a majority was ready for revision, the number was not as high as the figure stipulated by the Church's constitution.

William Greenough Thayer Shedd was one of the senior theologians of the Presbyterian Church who led the resistance to a revision of the Confession. His involvement in the controversy, and the publication of this book in 1893, was one of the last public episodes in his life. A New Englander, Shedd was born in Massachusetts on June 21, 1820. He graduated from the University of Vermont in 1839 and from Andover Theological Seminary in 1843. A two-year pastorate was followed by successive teaching appointments at Vermont, at Auburn Theological Seminary and in the chair of Church History at Andover (1853–1862). Shedd was out of sympathy with the doctrinal changes then occurring both at Andover and in New England in general and, from 1862, when he accepted a call to become associate Pastor (with Gardiner Spring) of the Brick Church in New York, he was to continue till his death as a Presbyterian minister. In the Presbyterian Church, writes John de Witt of Princeton

Shedd felt entirely at home. Not only was he a high and pronounced Calvinist; but he believed that a Church should be organized and committed to a system of religious truth; and that in its organization it should provide adequate means to secure the fidelity of its teachers to the system. He believed also that Calvinism leaves liberty enough to the preacher of the Gospel. And while he did not hold that the system is broad enough for the organization of the whole visible Church, he held that it was a theology broad enough to constitute the organizing principle of a denomination; and he believed that American history had already proved the value of denominational churches. That religious communions should be unified by systematic theology expressed in symbols, and not solely or chiefly by forms of government, he was strongly convinced; and he was not at all troubled by the fact that Calvinism organized, and so limited, the Church of which he was a minister. So he says: 'The Presbyterian Church is a Calvinistic Church, and it will be the beginning of its decline when it begins to swerve from this dogmatic position. The Westminster Confession, exactly as it now reads, has been the Creed of as free and enlarged intellects as ever lived on earth. The substance of it was the strong and fertile root of the two freest movements in modern history, that of the Protestant Reformation, and that of the Republican

Government. No Presbyterian should complain that the Creed of his Church is narrow and stifling.'[1]

After only a year at the Brick Church, New York, Dr. Shedd was appointed Professor of Biblical Literature in Union Theological Seminary, in the same city. His *Commentary on the Epistle to the Romans* is an example of the work which he did in this Chair before being transferred to the Professorship of Systematic Theology in 1874. This, his last post, he regarded as providing the most important work of his life. Two years before his resignation at the age of seventy (in 1890) he published the two volumes of his greatest work, *Dogmatic Theology*, and a third and supplementary volume was completed only two months before his death on Saturday, November 17, 1894.

Reporting the calmness and child-like confidence of his death, his pastor, Dr. Van Dyke, spoke of the comfort and strength which the older Christian then ministered to him: 'I thought then and still think, the subjects he talked about are the most sublime that ever engaged the thought or speech of man. They were the Holy Trinity and the eternal Kingdom of God. Once only, during the conversation, he spoke of his weakness and pain; and expressed the hope that "his release might not be long delayed".'[2]

Shedd did not live to see the outcome of the movement for credal change. The failure of the vote for revising the Confession in 1893 did not end the matter. A further revision committee was appointed by the General Assembly of 1900. This committee at length proposed three minor changes in the text of the Confession (leaving its system of doctrine unaffected) and also a Declaratory

---

[1]'William Greenough Thayer Shedd' in *The Presbyterian and Reformed Review*, April 1895, p 310.
[2]Quoted by John de Witt, *op. cit.*, p 321.

Statement which affirmed that Chapter III of the Confession, 'of God's Eternal Decree', was to be interpreted in harmony with the belief that God loves all mankind. These proposals passed the Assembly of 1903 and introduced, henceforth, a measure of ambiguity into the interpretation of the Confession. For B. B. Warfield, who had declined to serve on the revision committee, the Declaratory Statement was 'a body of loosely expressed sentences'. Along with Shedd and all the leaders who had resisted revision, Warfield did not deny the universality of God's love of benevolence, but, with his Princeton colleague, Geerhardus Vos, he argued that the divine love which is stressed in the Bible 'is not God's general benevolence, but His special affection for His people'. The Declaratory Statement, paralleled by similar statements of Presbyterian Churches in other parts of the world, simply spoke of 'love'. It left those who understood it in terms of 'benevolence' believing that the doctrine of the Confession was left unaffected, while others supposed that the old Calvinism had now been effectively modified and practically abandoned.

The subject of this book, it needs to be understood, is a much wider one than the above discussion may suggest. For virtually all branches of the Protestant churches, excepting the episcopal and the Wesleyan, the Westminster Confession and its Catechisms had been central in the doctrinal Christianity of the English-speaking world. In the Confession's understanding of redemption it long had the support of Congregationalists and Baptists, although the ministers of those denominations, unlike the Presbyterians, were not bound to its statements officially.

Such men as Shedd and Warfield were not against a revision of the Confession in principle. But they regarded the move to modify its Calvinism as arising from the spirit of the age rather than from any genuine advance in biblical understanding. The world of scholarship, at large, was hostile to the particularity of God's grace in redemption. Many of the revisionists believed that to rebuild theology upon the basis of universal love would win far broader support for Christianity. For Warfield, who declined to sit on the revision committee, it was 'an inexpressible grief' to see the Church 'spending its energies in a vain attempt to lower its testimony to suit the ever-changing sentiment of the world about it'. Of the Committee of Revision and its work, Warfield wrote in 1892

If there is a call for revision at all it is obviously for even clearer and more precise definition, for even higher and more finished construction, than the Westminster divines have given us in their noble formulation of the truth. New heresies have arisen; old heresies have won unexpected following. A sentence here and there, a section here and there, applying the old truth to the new conditions; bringing out the essential outlines of the eternal truth as over against the new heresies, so as to protect the Church from their insidious inroads; developing the structure of the old Reformed theology along its own essential and formative lines in the face of the new systems of error and in conquest over them – this might have been a revision worth making . . . To all the clamorous proclamation of false doctrine about us – yes, and in our midst – against which the Church needs protection, the Committee has been deaf. To all the demands thus made on it for progress in the doctrinal statement of our orthodox truth in relation to present-day needs, it has been blind. Turning its back on it all, its whole doctrinal work is comprised in requesting the Church to lower its voice in telling the world the truth! Let us face the situation frankly. These doctrines, our expression of which the Committee wishes us to modify and moderate, are true in their unmodified and unmoderated form. Their proclama-

tion is for the health of the world. We shall never pacify
the whale of error by throwing it this tub; or, as Mr.
Spurgeon put it in even sharper figure, we shall never
satisfy the pursuing wolves that seek to destroy our whole
system by flinging them our children to devour. The
Church would be more at her proper business in whet-
ting her weapons than in dulling them. It is not a time in
which to whisper the truth in doubtful phrases, but to
shout it from the housetops in the clearest and sharpest
language in which it can be framed. Distinctive Calvinism must be upheld against both Arminianism and the
subtler Arminianism which the German mediating
theology is giving such vogue among us; distinctive
Augustinianism, against semi-Pelagianism and the subtler semi-Pelagianism of Thomism and Tridentinism, the
barriers against which the suggested alterations in our
expression of the doctrine of sin break down. Let him
that is fearful and trembling, indeed, return and depart.
But though there be but a Gideon's hundred left, if they
will take but their lights in their hands, and break their
pitchers that the lights may shine, and blow with their
trumpets and shout THE SWORD OF THE LORD!, the
sword of the Lord will get them the victory.[1]

Today, nearly a hundred years after this forgotten controversy, the issue about which Shedd writes is again to the
fore. The Westminster Confession is being sold and read,
in various editions, around the world to an extent which
would have been regarded by many as unthinkable fifty
years ago. Yet this ought not to be surprising because,
ultimately, there can be only two alternatives in an evangelical understanding of the Christian Faith, the Calvinistic
and the Arminian. The Church has passed through an era in
which the Arminian understanding has held sway and its
effects in evangelism, in worship and in Christian living

[1] 'The Final Report of the Revision Committee', *The Presbyterian and
Reformed Review*, April 1892, pp 329–330.

have had opportunity to be worked out fully. We are again, in history, at a turning point. Increasing numbers have come to see that these two systems are irreconcilably different and that no small part of the failures of the churches in the English-speaking world in the present century is connected with the displacement of the doctrine of Protestantism's foremost confessional statement.

This book has long been one of the rarest of Shedd's volumes. We can well believe that it may have wider influence today than at its first publication. To set the theme in its wider context we have added to this reprint a summary of an address by his friend and fellow-labourer, B. B. Warfield, on 'The Significance of the Westminster Standards as a Creed'. It was Warfield who announced simultaneously the death of 'two of the greatest Presbyterians of our generation', James McCosh of Princeton and W. G. T. Shedd, in *The Presbyterian and Reformed Review* for January 1895. Of these two men he wrote:

> Each had been given a message to deliver, and had delivered it. Each had been called upon to champion the cause of truth against serious odds, and had not shunned the task. 'They never sold the truth to serve the hour' . . . Dr. Shedd was a noble preacher, and admirable teacher of an unusually wide range of subjects, a man of letters, an accomplished scholar, a philosophic thinker: but above all he was a great theologian. Both men had the clearness of vision to discern reality in philosophy or religion: both had the courage, on discerning it, to grasp and to hold it for themselves and for us. They have embalmed not their memories only, but their teaching also, for us in a somewhat voluminous literary product to which we shall increasingly feel our debt.[1]

[1] *The Presbyterian and Reformed Review*, Jan 1895, p 123. Articles by Warfield against revision of the Confession will be found listed at the front of his volume, *The Westminster Assembly and Its Work*, 1931.

1: *Inexpediency of the Revision of the Westminster Confession.*[1]

The question whether the Westminster Confession shall be revised has been referred to the whole Church represented by the presbyteries. The common sentiment of the denomination must determine the matter. The expression of opinion during the few months prior to the presbyterial action is, therefore, of consequence. It is desirable that it should be a full expression of all varieties of views, and as a contribution towards it, we purpose to assign some reasons why the revision of the Confession is not expedient.

1. In the first place it is inexpedient, because in its existing form as drawn up by the Westminster Assembly it has met, and well met, all the needs of the Church for the past two centuries. The Presbyterian Church in the United States since 1700 has passed through a varied and sometimes difficult experience. The controversies in the beginning between the Old and New Lights, and still more the vehement disputes that resulted in the division of the Church in 1837, have tried the common symbol as severely as it is ever likely to be. But through them all both theological divisions were content with the Confession and Catechisms as they stood, and both alike claimed to be true to them. Neither party demanded a revision on any doctrinal points; and both alike found in

[1]New York Evangelist, September 5, 1889.

them a satisfactory expression of their faith. What is there in the Presbyterian Church of to-day that necessitates any different statement of the doctrine of decrees, of atonement, of regeneration, or of punishment, from that accepted by the Presbyterian Church of 1837, or 1789? Are the statements upon these points any more liable to misconception or misrepresentation by non-Calvinists now than they were fifty or a hundred years ago? Are there any more 'weak consciences' requiring softening explanations and relaxing clauses in the Church of to-day than in former periods? And with reference to the allowable differences of theological opinion within the Presbyterian Church, is not a creed that was adopted and defended by Charles Hodge and Albert Barnes sufficiently broad to include all who are really Calvinistic and Presbyterian in belief? What is there, we repeat, in the condition of the Presbyterian Church of to-day that makes the old Confession of the past two hundred years inadequate as a doctrinal Standard? All the past successes and victories of Presbyterianism have been accomplished under it. Success in the past is guaranty for success in the future. Is it not better for the Church to work on the very same old base, in the very same straight line?

2. Revision is inexpedient, because the reunion of the two divisions of the Church was founded upon the Confession as it now stands. A proposition to unite the two branches of Presbyterianism by first revising the Westminster documents would have failed, because in the revision individual and party preferences would have shown themselves. But when the Standards pure and simple were laid down as the only terms of union, the whole mass of Presbyterians flowed together. It is to be feared that if a revision of the Confession should take place, there will be a dissatisfied portion of the Church

who will prefer to remain upon the historic foundation; that the existing harmony will be disturbed; and that the proposed measures for union with other Presbyterian bodies will fall through.

3. Revision is inexpedient, because it will introduce new difficulties. The explanations will need to be explained. The revision that is called for is said by its more conservative advocates, not to be an alteration of the doctrine of the Confession, but an explanation only. Now *good* and *sufficient* explanations of a creed require more space than can be afforded in a concise symbol intended for use in inducting officers and members. Such full and careful explanations have been made all along from the beginning, and the Presbyterian Board of Publication has issued a large and valuable library of them. No one need be in any doubt respecting the meaning of the Confession who will carefully peruse one or more of them. He who is not satisfied with the Westminster doctrine as so explained, will not be satisfied with it at all. But if brief explanations are inserted into the Confession itself, their brevity will inevitably expose them to misunderstanding and misconception. Take an illustration. An able minister and divine, whose Calvinism is unimpeachable, suggests that Confession iii. 3 shall read: 'By the decree of God, for the manifestation of his glory, some men and angels are predestinated unto everlasting life, and others foreordained [for their sins] to everlasting death'. If the clause in brackets is inserted without further explanation, the article might fairly and naturally be understood to teach that the reason why God passes by a sinner in the bestowment of regenerating grace is the sinner's sin. But St. Paul expressly says that the sinner's sin is not the cause of his non-election to regeneration. 'The children being not yet born, neither having done any good or evil, it was said, The elder shall serve the younger. Esau have I hated'

[3]

(*Rom. 9: 11–13*). The reason for the difference between the elect and non-elect is not the holiness or the sin of either of them, but God's sovereign good pleasure. 'He hath mercy on whom he will have mercy, and whom he will he hardeneth' (*Rom. 9: 18*). An explanation like this, without further explanation such as the proposer would undoubtedly make, would not only contradict Scripture, but change the Calvinistic doctrine into the Arminian. The reason for non-election would no longer be secret and sovereign, but known and conditional. All this liability to misconstruction is avoided by the Confession itself as it now stands. For in Confession iii. 7, after saying that the 'passing by' in the bestowment of regenerating grace is an act of God's sovereign pleasure, 'whereby he extendeth or withholdeth mercy as he pleaseth', it then adds that 'the *ordaining to dishonor and wrath*' is 'for sin.' Sin is here represented as the reason for the judicial act of punishing, but not for the sovereign act of not regenerating. The only reason for the latter, our Lord gives in his 'Even so, Father, for so it seemed good in thy sight'.

Other illustrations might be given of the difficulty of avoiding misconception when a systematic creed is sought to be explained, particularly in its difficult points, by the brief interpolation of words and clauses. The method is too short. More space is required than can be spared. It is better, therefore, to let a carefully constructed and concisely phrased creed like the Westminster stand exactly as it was drawn up by the sixty-nine commissioners, in the five weekly sessions for nearly nine years, and have it explained, qualified, and defended in published treatises, in sermons, and especially in catechetical lectures. Had the ministry been as faithful as it should in years past in catechetical instruction, there would be little difficulty in understanding the Westminster creed. The remedy needed is in this direction, not in that of a revision.

4. Revision is inexpedient, because there is no end to the process. It is like the letting out of water. The doctrine of the divine decrees is the particular one selected by the presbytery whose request has brought the subject of revision before the General Assembly. But this doctrine runs entirely through the Westminster documents, so that if changes were made merely in the third chapter of the Confession, it would be wholly out of harmony with the remainder. Effectual calling, regeneration, perseverance of the saints, are all linked in with the divine decree. The most cursory perusal will show that a revision of the Confession on this one subject would amount to an entire recasting of the creed.

5. Revision is inexpedient, because it may abridge the liberty of interpretation now afforded by the Confession. As an example of the variety in explanation admitted by the creed as it now stands, take the statement that 'God the Father, Son, and Holy Ghost, in the beginning, created or made from nothing the world, and all things therein, in the space of six days'. He who holds the patristic view that the days of Genesis were periods, and he who holds the modern opinion that the days were solar, can subscribe to the Westminster statement. But if revised in the interest of either view, the subscriber is shut up to it alone. Another example is found in the statement respecting the guilt of Adam's sin. The advocate of natural union, or of representative union, or of both in combination, can find a foothold, provided only that he holds to the *penal* nature of the first sin. Another instance is the article concerning 'elect infants'. As the tenet was formulated by the Assembly, it has been understood to mean, (a) that all infants dying in infancy are elected as a class, some being saved by covenanted mercy, and some by uncovenanted mercy; (b) that all infants dying in infancy are elected as a class – all alike, those within the Church and those outside

of it, being saved by divine mercy, nothing being said of the covenant; (c) that dying infants are elected as individuals, some being elect, and some non-elect. Probably each of these opinions had its representatives in the Assembly, and hence the indefinite form of the statement. The writer regards the first-mentioned view as best supported by Scripture and the analogy of faith; but there are many who advocate the second view, and perhaps there may be some who hold the third. The liberty of opinion now conceded by the Confession on a subject respecting which the Scripture data are few, would be ill-exchanged for a statement that would admit of but one interpretation.

6. Revision is inexpedient, because the Westminster Confession, as it now reads, is a sufficiently broad and liberal creed. We do not say that it is sufficiently broad and liberal for every man and every denomination; but it is as broad and liberal for a Calvinist as any Calvinist should desire. For whoever professes Calvinism, professes a precise form of doctrine. He expects to keep within definite metes and bounds; he is not one of those religionists who start from no premises, and come to no conclusions, and hold no tenets. The Presbyterian Church is a Calvinistic Church. It will be the beginning of its decline, as it already has been of some Calvinistic denominations, when it begins to swerve from this dogmatic position. It must therefore be distinguished among the Churches for doctrinal consistency, comprehensiveness, and firmness. But inside of the metes and bounds established by divine revelation, and to which it has voluntarily confined itself, it has a liberty that is as large as the kingdom of God. It cannot get outside of that kingdom, and should not desire to. But within it, it is as free to career as a ship in the ocean, as an eagle in the air. Yet the ship cannot sail beyond the ocean, nor the eagle fly beyond the sky. Liberty within the immeasurable bounds and limits of God's truth, is the

only true liberty. All else is license. The Westminster Confession, exactly as it now reads, has been the creed of as free and enlarged intellects as ever lived on earth. The substance of it was the strong and fertile root of the two freest movements in modern history: that of the Protestant Reformation and that of Republican Government. No Presbyterian should complain that the creed of his Church is narrow and stifling.

And here we notice an objection urged against the Confession relative to the tenet of limited redemption. It is said that it is not sufficiently broad and liberal in announcing the boundless compassion of God towards all men indiscriminately, and in inviting all men without exception to cast themselves upon it. But read and ponder the following statements:

'Repentance unto life is an evangelical grace, the doctrine whereof is to be preached in season and out of season by every minister of the gospel, as well as that of faith in Christ. It is every man's duty to endeavor to repent of his particular sins, particularly. Every man is bound to make private confession of his sins to God, praying for the pardon thereof, upon which, and the forsaking of them, he shall find mercy. Prayer, with thanksgiving, being one special part of religious worship, is by God required of all men. Prayer is to be made for all sorts of men living, or that shall live hereafter, but not for the dead. God is to be worshipped everywhere in spirit and in truth, and in secret each one by himself. God in his Word, by a positive moral commandment, binds all men in all ages. The grace of God is manifested in the second covenant, in that he freely provideth and offereth to sinners a mediator, and life and salvation in him. The ministry of the gospel testifies that whosoever believes in Christ shall be saved, and excludes none that will come unto him. God is able to search the heart, hear the requests, pardon the sins, and fulfil the desires, of all.'

These declarations, scattered broadcast through the Westminster Confession and Catechisms, teach the universality of the gospel, except no human creature from the offer of it, and exclude no human creature from its benefits. Their consistency with the doctrine of election is assumed, but not explained, in the Confession of Faith. And no revision of this by the mere interpolation of a few words or clauses, will make the subject any clearer, or stop all objections.

7. Revision is inexpedient, because the Westminster Standards already make full provision for those exceptional cases, on account of which revision is claimed by its advocates to be needed. It is said that there are some true believers in the Lord Jesus Christ, who cannot adopt all the Westminster statements, who yet should not be, and actually are not, excluded from the Presbyterian Church; that there are tender consciences of good men, whose scruples are to be respected. But these cases are referred by the Form of Government to the church session, and power is given to it to receive into membership any person who trusts in the blood of Christ for the remission of sin, although his doctrinal knowledge and belief may be unsatisfactory on some points. He may stumble at predestination, but if with the publican he cries 'God be merciful to me a sinner', he has the root of the matter in him, and is a regenerate child of God. But why should the whole Presbyterian Church revise its entire creed, so as to make it fit these exceptional cases? Why should the mountain go to Mohammed? Why should a genuine but deficient evangelical knowledge and experience be set up as the type of doctrine for the whole denomination? These 'babes in Christ' need the education of the full and complete system of truth, and should gradually be led up to it, instead of bringing the system down to their level.

There is sometimes a misconception at this point. We have seen it stated that the membership of the Presbyterian Church is not required or expected to hold the same doctrine with the officers; that the pastor, elders, and deacons must accept the Confession of Faith 'as containing the system of doctrine taught in the Holy Scriptures', but that the congregation need not. But this error arises from confounding the toleration of a deficiency with the endorsement of it. Because a church session tolerates in a particular person, who gives evidence of faith in Christ, an error respecting foreordination, or even some abstruse point in the Trinity, or the incarnation, it does not thereby endorse the error. It does not sanction his opinion on these subjects, but only endures it, in view of his religious experience on the vital points of faith and repentance, and with the hope that his subsequent growth in knowledge will bring him to the final rejection of it. The Presbyterian Church tolerates theatre-going in some of its members: that is to say, it does not discipline them for it. But it does not formally approve of and sanction theatre-going. A proposition to revise the Confession by inserting a clause to this effect, in order to meet the wishes and practice of theatre-going church-members, would be voted down by the presbyteries.

The position that the officers of a church may have one creed, and the membership another, is untenable. No church could live and thrive upon it. A Trinitarian clergy preaching to an Arian or Socinian membership, would preach to unwilling hearers. And although the difference is not so great and so vital, yet a Calvinistic clergy preaching to an Arminian membership, or an Arminian clergy to a Calvinistic membership, would on some points find unsympathetic auditors. Pastor and people, officers and members, must be homogeneous in doctrine, in order to a vigorous church-life. If, therefore, a certain class of members is received into a church, who do not on all points agree with the Church creed, this is not to be understood as giving the members generally a liberty to depart from the Church creed, or to be a reason for revising it.[1]

The case is different with the officers of the church. There is *no exceptional class* in this instance. Neither the session nor the presbytery have any authority to dispense with the acceptance of any part of the Confession of Faith, when a pastor, elder, or deacon is inducted into office. There is no toleration of defective views provided for, when those who are to teach and rule the Church are put into the ministry. And this for the good reason that ministers and elders are expected to be so well indoctrinated, that they are 'apt to teach' and competent to 'rule well'. Some propose 'loose subscription' as a remedy, when candidates of lax or unsettled views present themselves for licensure and ordination. This is demoralizing, and kills all simplicity and godly sincerity. Better a thousand times for a denomination to alter its creed, than to allow its ministry to 'palter with words in a double meaning'; than to permit an Arian subscription to the Nicene Symbol, an Arminian subscription to the Westminster Confession, a Calvinistic subscription to the Articles of Wesley, a Restorationist subscription to the doctrine of endless punishment.

For these reasons, it seems to us that the proposed revision of the Westminster Confession is not wise or expedient. The revision of a denominational creed is a rare occurrence in ecclesiastical history. Commonly a denom-

---

[1]The question whether there shall be a short creed to be used in the admission of members into the Church, is entirely distinct from that of revision. Such a creed ought not, of course, to contain anything *contradictory* to the larger creed which makes a part of the constitution of the Church, and is used in the induction of ministers, elders, and theological professors.

ination remains from first to last upon the base that was laid for it in the beginning by its fathers and founders. And when revision does occur, it is seldom in the direction of fulness and precision. Usually the alteration is in favor of vague and looser statements. Even slight changes are apt to be followed by greater ones. The disposition to revise and alter, needs watching. In an age when the general drift of the unregenerate world is away from the strong statements of the Hebrew prophets, of Christ and his inspired Apostles, it is of the utmost importance that the regenerate Church, in all its denominations, should stand firm in the old paths, and hold fast to that 'Word of God which is sharper than a two-edged sword, piercing even to the dividing asunder of soul and spirit'.

2: *Objections to the Revision of the Westminster Confession.*[1]

The first question sent down to the presbyteries is the more important of the two; namely, Whether a revision of the Confession is desired. If this is answered in the negative, it will mean that the Presbyterian Church of the present day is satisfied with its ancestral faith, as formulated in its Standards, and accords with the Church of the past in this respect. It will be a formal and positive *reaffirmation* of the historic Calvinism, at a time when this system of doctrine is charged with being unscriptural, erroneous, and antiquated by modern theological progress. If it be answered in the affirmative, it will mean that the Church of the present day is more or less dissatisfied with the doctrines of the Westminster Assembly, and is no longer willing to endorse and preach them as that body of divines defined and stated them. Revision is *alteration*, more or less. The object is not merely to make sure that the creed just as it stands is understood; but to modify it either in its structural plan, its component parts, its emphasis, or its general perspective. The second question, How much revision is desired? is comparatively of less consequence, because it is the first question alone that decides the vital point, whether the Presbyterian Church has drifted at all from the old anchorage. For this reason,

[1] New York Presbytery, November 20, 1889; Northwestern Presbyterian, November 23, 1889.

we present in a brief form the following objections to the revision of the Westminster Confession:

1. Revision is objectionable, because the project originated in too small a fraction of the Church. Only fifteen presbyteries out of two hundred and two united in overturing the Assembly in its favor. The remaining one hundred and eighty-seven will have to be argued and persuaded into it. But so important a step as the revision of the doctrinal basis of a denomination should begin in a general uprising of the whole body, and be the spontaneous and strongly expressed desire of the great majority of its members. The revision of secondary matters, like the form of government and discipline, does not require this in the same degree. As the case now stands, fifteen presbyteries have asked one hundred and eighty-seven presbyteries if they do not want to amend the Confession. There should have been a far wider dissatisfaction with the Standards than this indicates, to initiate revision.

2. Revision is objectionable, because the Confession is a correct statement of 'the system of doctrine contained in the Scriptures'. The system meant in this phrase is universally known as the Calvinistic; not as resting upon the authority of Calvin, but as a convenient designation of that interpretation of Scripture which is common to Augustine, Calvin, the Reformed theologians, and the Westminster divines. The term 'evangelical' does not define it, because there are several evangelical systems, but only one Calvinistic. The systems of Arminius, of Wesley, and of the Later-Lutherans, as well as that of Calvin, are alike evangelical, in distinction from anti-evangelical systems like Socinianism and Deism. They are all alike derived from the Bible, and contain the doctrines of the Trinity, the incarnation, the apostasy, and the redemption. But the Calvinistic interpretation of Scripture, which is the one formulated in the Westminster

[13]

Standards, differs from these other 'evangelical' systems, in teaching unconditional election and preterition, instead of conditional; limited redemption (not atonement) instead of unlimited; regeneration wholly by the Holy Spirit instead of partly; the total inability of the sinner instead of partial. The Calvinistic system, as thus discriminated from the other 'evangelical' systems, has been adopted by American Presbyterians for two centuries. Neither Old Lights, nor New Lights; neither Old School, nor New School; have demanded that these tenets which distinguish Calvinism from Arminianism should be eliminated from the creed. They were accepted with equal sincerity by both branches of the Church in the reunion of 1870, and there is no reason for altering the formulas that were satisfactory then, unless the belief of the Church has altered in regard to these distinctive points of Calvinism.

3. The revision of the Confession is objectionable, because the principal amendments proposed by its advocates will introduce error into it, so that it will no longer be 'the system of doctrine contained in the Scriptures.' The four following alterations are urged upon the Church: (a) To strike out the doctrine of the sovereignty of God in preterition, leaving the doctrine of election unlimited and universal. (b) To retain preterition, but assign as the reason for it the sin of the non-elect. (c) To strike out the statement that the number of the elect and non-elect is 'so certain and definite, that it cannot be increased or diminished' by 'angels and men'. (d) To strike out the statement that no man who rejects the 'Christian religion', or the evangelical method of salvation, can be saved by the legal method of living 'according to the light of nature', or some system of morality which he 'professes'. If these changes are made, the Westminster Standards will no longer contain a class of truths that are plainly taught in Scripture, and will cease to be that

'system of doctrine' which their authors had in mind, and to which the present generation of ministers and elders have subscribed like their fathers before them.

4. Revision is objectionable, because it will be a concession to the enemies of the Standards that their aspersions of them are true. The charges that have been made by the opponents of them from time immemorial are, that Calvinism represents God as a tyrannical sovereign who is destitute of love and mercy for any but an elect few, that it attributes to man the depravity of devils, deprives him of moral freedom, and subjects him to the arbitrary cruelty of a Being who creates some men in order to damn them. A few ministers and elders within the Presbyterian Church endorse these allegations; and many assert that the Confession contains no universal offer of salvation, teaches that none of the heathen are saved, and that some infants are non-elect and lost. The great reason assigned by such Presbyterians for revising the Standards is, that they inculcate unscriptural and offensive doctrines that cannot be believed or preached. But this is to concede that all preceding Presbyterians have been grossly mistaken in denying that the Confession contains such doctrines, either directly or by implication. It is an acknowledgment that one of the most carefully drawn and important of all the Reformed symbols, inculcates in a latent form some of the most repulsive tenets conceivable by the human mind. Presbyterians of all schools have hitherto met this calumny on their creed by contradicting it, and trying the issue by close reasoning and debate. Revision proposes, in the legal phrase, to give a cognovit, admit the charge, and alter the standards to suit the enemy who made it.

5. Revision is objectionable, because it will reopen the old discussions and controversies upon the difficult doctrines, without resulting in any better definitions of

them than they already have in the Church. On the contrary, the great variety of changes that will be urged, from the very conservative to the very radical, will introduce a period of speculative dispute and disagreement that will seriously impair the existing harmony of the denomination, and divert its attention from the great practical interests of Christ's kingdom in which it is now engaged.

These five objections, it seems to us, are conclusive reasons why the Presbyterian Church should not *alter*, but *reaffirm* the doctrines of the Westminster Standards, and continue to teach and defend them as they have been by all the past generations of Presbyterians.

3: *Are There Doctrinal Errors in the West-minster Confession?*[1]

The strongest reason presented for the revision of the Westminster Confession is the allegation that the phraseology of some of its sections contains serious error, or is liable to be understood as containing it. Is this true? In order to answer this question, we shall examine a few of the principal sections which are asserted to be erroneous either in their direct teaching or in their implication.

1. Confession iii. 3 asserts that 'By the decree of God, for the manifestation of his glory, some men and angels are predestinated unto everlasting life, and others foreordained to everlasting death'. It is contended that this section teaches, or is liable to be understood as teaching, that the decree of God in election and reprobation has no connection with sin and the fall of man, but that God by an arbitrary decree, wholly irrespective of sin, creates some men in order to save them, and some men in order to damn them. To correct this alleged error, or liability of interpretation, several advocates of revision propose to insert the clause, 'On account of their sins', to qualify the clause, 'Foreordained to everlasting death;' and one advocate of revision proposes to strike out the entire section concerning election and reprobation.

We maintain that the Confession neither teaches the

[1]Philadelphia Presbyterian, October 19, 1889.

error aforesaid, nor is fairly liable to be understood to teach it. According to Confession iii. 6, both the elect and non-elect are 'fallen in Adam', and are thereby in a common guilty state of sin. The former are delivered out of sin by regenerating grace, and the latter are left in sin. Why are the latter left in sin? Because 'God so pleased', is the reason given by the Confession. 'On account of their sins', is the reason which the reviser would insert into the Confession. But this, surely, cannot be the reason why God *leaves* a sinner in his sin. I see two suicides who have flung themselves into the water. I rescue one of them, and the other I let drown. They are both alike in the water, and by their own free agency. But his being in the water, is not the reason why I do not rescue the one whom I let drown. I have some other reason. It may be a good one or a bad one. But whatever it be, it certainly is not because the man is in the water. Similarly God does not leave a sinner in his own voluntary and loved sin because he is in sin. He has some other reason why he makes this discrimination between two persons, both of whom are in sin, neither of whom has any claim upon his mercy, and neither of whom is more deserving of election and regeneration than the other. God's reason, in this case, we know must be a good one. But it is a secret with himself. The only answer to the inquiry, 'Why didst thou elect and regenerate Saul of Tarsus, and didst not elect and regenerate Judas Iscariot?' is, 'Because it seemed good in my sight'.

The allegation that there is error in this section of the Confession arises from misunderstanding the meaning of the clause, 'Foreordained to everlasting death'. It is the *omission to regenerate*, not the *punishment of sin*, that is intended by it. When God 'foreordains' a sinner 'to everlasting death', he decides to leave him in the sin which deserves everlasting death and results in it. The non-elect sinner has experienced the operation of common grace. It is an error to say that God shows no kind or degree of mercy to the non-elect. But he has resisted and defeated it. God decides to proceed no further with him by the bestowment of that special grace which regenerates, and 'makes willing in the day of God's power'. The elect sinner has also experienced, resisted, and defeated common grace. God decides to proceed further with him, by effectual calling and regeneration. The particular question, therefore, in this paragraph of the Confession is, 'Why does God *leave* a sinner to his own wilful free agency?' and not, 'Why does God *punish* him for it?' The answer to the first question is, 'Because of his sovereign good pleasure'. The answer to the second is, 'Because of the ill-desert of sin'. The reason why God omits to take the second step, and exert a yet higher degree of grace after his first step in exerting a lower degree has been thwarted by the resistance of the sinner, is entirely different from the reason why he inflicts retribution upon the sinner's sin. This is more fully explained in the seventh section of the third chapter, which should always be read in connection with the third. Here, the reason for God's 'passing by', or omitting to regenerate a sinner, is found in 'the unsearchable counsel of his own will whereby he extendeth or withholdeth mercy as he pleaseth'. This first negative part of reprobation, which is properly called 'preterition', is not qualified by the clause, 'for their sin', as the correct punctuation in the Board's edition shows. This latter clause qualifies only the sentence, 'And to ordain them to dishonor and wrath'. Sinners are *punished* 'for their sin', but sin is not the reason why God *does not regenerate* them. If sin were the reason for non-election, holiness, logically, would be the reason for election. If some men are not regenerated because they are unbelieving, others would be regenerated because they are believing. This is the Arminian doctrine, not the Calvinistic; and this is the reason why the Westminster Assembly did *not* qualify the words, 'pass by', by the proposed clause, 'for their sins', but left 'passing by', or 'foreordination to everlasting death', to be a purely sovereign act according to 'the good pleasure' of God.

2. Confession iii. 4 teaches that 'the angels and men thus predestinated and foreordained are particularly and unchangeably designed; and their number is so certain and definite that it cannot be either increased or diminished'. One advocate of revision proposes that this whole section be struck out of the Standards, because it 'is not a scriptural form of expression; it is misleading'.

What is the meaning of this section? 'Increased or diminished' by *whom*? What is the ellipsis intended to be supplied by the framers of the statement? Plainly they meant that the number of the elect and non-elect cannot be increased or diminished by the 'angels and men' spoken of in the connection: that is, by any finite power. Neither the human will, nor the angelic, can determine the number of God's elect and non-elect, because this depends wholly upon 'the counsel of his own will'. Of course, the Assembly did not mean to say that *God* could not have made the number of his elect larger or smaller, if 'the counsel of his own will' had so determined. Probably no advocate of revision understands the Confession to teach this. But will any advocate of it say that the number of the regenerate and saved can be made greater or less by the decision and action of either the unregenerate world, or the regenerate church? This would contradict the statement of St. John, that the elect 'sons of God are born not of blood, nor of the will of the flesh, nor of the will of man, but of God'. It would also contradict the corresponding statement in the Confession which teaches that 'in effectual calling man is altogether passive, until being quickened and renewed by the Holy Spirit, he is thereby enabled to answer the call, and to embrace the grace offered and conveyed by it' (Confession x. 2). This fourth section of the third chapter is simply another way of teaching the common doctrine, running all through the Standards, that the sinful will is in *bondage* to sin, and cannot regenerate itself, and that consequently the number of the regenerate depends wholly upon the will and decision of God.

3. Confession x. 4 asserts that 'men not professing the Christian religion cannot be saved in any other way whatsoever, be they never so diligent to frame their lives according to the light of nature, and the law of that religion they do profess'. This is alleged to be erroneous by an advocate of revision, because 'every promise and every warning of God is addressed to man as a free agent, and not as one who cannot be saved'.

Who are the persons 'not professing the Christian religion?' They are those who *reject* it, either formally, or in their spirit and disposition. The class here spoken of are the *legalists* of every variety, who repudiate salvation through Christ's blood and righteousness, and rely upon 'diligently framing their lives according to the light of nature, and the law of that religion which they do profess' – which is some other than 'the Christian religion', which they do not 'profess', but condemn. The Christian religion is evangelical religion, and this they dislike. They expect to be saved by morality and personal virtue, and not by faith in the vicarious atonement of Jesus Christ.

The doctrine then, in this section is, in brief, that no man can be saved by good works; by any endeavors however 'diligent' to obey the written law of the decalogue, as the Christian legalist does, or the unwritten law of conscience, as the heathen legalist does. Now concerning this class of persons St. Paul explicitly says that 'they cannot be saved'. 'By the deeds of the law shall no flesh be justified'. St. Peter says the same. 'There is no other name under heaven given among men, whereby we must be saved'.

There is nothing in this section that denies the possibility of the salvation of any sinner on earth who feels his sin, and trusts in the sacrifice of Christ in case he has heard of it, or *would* trust in it if he should hear of it. It does not teach that no heathen is or can be saved. This fourth section, so often misunderstood and misrepresented, is aimed at the self-righteous moralist, whether in Christendom or Heathendom, who has no sorrow for sin, feels no need of God's mercy as manifested in Christ, and has no disposition to cast himself upon it, but claims the rewards of eternity on the ground of personal character and obedience to 'the light of nature' and the maxims of morality. It is only a bold and strong assertion of the great truth, that no sinner can be saved by his most strenuous endeavors to keep the moral law. It is not strange, therefore, that this section closes with the affirmation that 'to assert and maintain the contrary is very pernicious and to be detested'.

If this is the correct explanation of these three sections of the Confession, it is evident that they neither teach nor imply error, and therefore do not need any revision.

4: *The Westminster Standards and the Universal Offer of Mercy.*[1]

The Westminster Standards are now meeting an attack from some who have adopted them as their religious creed. Formerly the onset came from the enemy on the outside, now it comes from within the Church. When so many presbyterians are objecting to the Confession as containing 'offensive articles that wound the consciences of tens of thousands of loyal and orthodox presbyterians', it is proper for an ordinary presbyterian to say a good word for the time-honored symbol which has been subscribed by the present generation of ministers and elders, and was dear to all the former generations. May it not be that these 'offensive articles' are not in the Standards, and that the advocates of revision, in order to find a sufficient reason for their project, are inventing and fighting men of straw? Let us look at one of these alleged offences.

It is strenuously contended that the Standards contain no declaration of the love of God towards all men, but limit it to the elect; that they make no universal offer of salvation, but confine it to a part of mankind.

The following declaration is found in Confession ii. 1.

'There is but one only living and true God, who is most loving, gracious, merciful, long suffering, abundant in goodness and truth, forgiving iniquity, transgression and

[1]New York Observer, November 14, 1889.

sin, the rewarder of them that diligently seek him.' Of whom speaketh the Confession this? Of the God of the elect only? Or of the God of every man? Is he the God of the elect only? Is he not also of the non-elect? Is this description of the gracious nature and attributes of God intended to be restricted to a part of mankind? Is not God as thus delineated the Creator and Father of every man without exception? Can it be supposed that the authors of this statement meant to be understood to say that God is not such a being for all men, but only for some? If this section does not teach the unlimited love and compassion of God towards all men as men, as his creatures, it teaches nothing.

The following declaration is found in Confession xv. 1, Larger Catechism, 159. 'Repentance unto life is an evangelical grace, the doctrine whereof is to be preached in season and out of season by every minister of the gospel, as well as that of faith in Christ.' This certainly teaches that faith and repentance are the duty of all men, not of some only. No one contends that the Confession teaches that God has given a limited command to repent. 'God commandeth all men everywhere to repent.' But how could he give such a universal command to all sinners if he is not willing to pardon all sinners? if his benevolent love is confined to some sinners in particular? How could our Lord command his ministers to preach the doctrine of faith and repentance to 'every creature', if he does not desire that every one of them would believe and repent? And how can he desire this if he does not feel infinite love for the souls of all? When the Confession teaches the duty of universal faith and repentance, it teaches by necessary inference the doctrine of God's universal compassion and readiness to forgive. And it also teaches in the same inferential way, that the sacrifice of Christ for sin is ample for the forgiveness of every man. To preach the duty of immediate belief on the Lord Jesus Christ as obligatory upon every man, in connection with the doctrine imputed to the Confession by the reviser, that God feels compassion for only the elect, and that Christ's sacrifice is not sufficient for all, would be self-contradictory. The two things cannot be put together. The reviser misunderstands the Standards, and reads into them a false doctrine that is not there.

Confession xv. 5, 6, declares that 'it is every man's duty to endeavor to repent of his particular sins particularly. Every man is bound to make private confession of his sins to God, praying for the pardon thereof, upon which, and the forsaking of them, he shall find mercy'. How shall every such man find mercy, if the reviser's understanding of the Confession is correct? if it teaches that God's love for sinners is limited to the elect, and that Christ's sacrifice is not sufficient for the sins of all? According to the revised version, the meaning of the Westminster divines in this section is, that some men who 'pray for pardon and forsake sin' shall 'find mercy', and some shall not.

Larger Catechism, 160, declares that 'it is required of those that hear the word preached, that they attend upon it with diligence, preparation and prayer; receive the truth in faith, love, meekness and readiness of mind, as the word of God; hide it in their hearts, and bring forth the fruit of it in their lives'. Would God require all this from every hearer of the word, if he were not kindly disposed towards him? if he did not love and pity his immortal soul, and desire its salvation? Does not this declaration mean that God will encourage, assist, and bless every hearer of the word without exception who does the things mentioned? What shadow of reason is there for alleging that it means that God will help and bless some of these hearers, and some he will not? But in order to make out that the section does not teach the universal offer of mercy, this must be the allegation.

Larger Catechism, 95, declares that 'the moral law is of use to all men, to inform them of the holy nature and will of God; to convince them of their disability to keep it, and of the sinful pollution of their nature; to humble them in the sense of sin and misery, and thereby help them to a clearer sight of the need they have of Christ, and of the perfection of his obedience'. But what is the use of showing every man his need of Christ, if Christ's sacrifice is not sufficient for every man? What reason is there for convincing every man of the pollution of his nature, and humbling him for it, unless God is for every man 'most loving, gracious, merciful, long-suffering, forgiving iniquity, transgression and sin?' The doctrine taught in this section, that all men are to be convicted of sin, like the doctrine that all men are to repent and to pray, supposes that God sustains a common benevolent and merciful relation to them all.

Confession xxi. 3, declares that 'prayer with thanksgiving, being one special part of religious worship, is required by God of all men'. How could God require prayer from every man, if he were not disposed to hear the prayer of every man? And does not this imply that he loves the soul of every man? The duty of prayer supposes a corresponding kind and gracious feeling in God that prompts him to answer it; that 'he is the hearer of prayer, and that unto him all flesh should come'. In order to make out his 'offensive doctrine', the reviser must explain this section by appending to it: 'Though God requires prayer from all men, he is the hearer of prayer for only the elect'.

Confession vii. 3, declares that 'man by his fall having made himself incapable of life by that (legal) covenant, the Lord was pleased to make a second, commonly called the covenant of grace: wherein he freely offered to sinners life and salvation by Jesus Christ, requiring of them faith in him, that they may be saved, and promising to give unto all those that are ordained unto life, his Holy Spirit, to make them willing and able to believe'. Two distinct and different things are mentioned here: (a) an offer of salvation; (b) a promise of the Holy Spirit to make the unwilling sinner willing to accept it. The number of those to whom the offer of salvation is made is unlimited; of those to whom the promise of the Spirit to 'make them willing' is made, is limited by 'ordination to life' or election. It is clear that God may desire that to be done by man under the influence of his common grace in the common call, which he may not decide and purpose to *make* him do by the operation of his special grace in the effectual call. His desire that sinners would hear his universal call to repentance may be, and is unlimited; but his purpose to overcome their unwillingness and incline them to repentance may be, and is limited. God offers Christ's sacrifice to every man, without exception, and assures him that if he will trust in it he shall be saved, and gives him common grace to help and encourage him to believe. This is a proof that God loves his soul and desires its salvation. But God does not, in addition to this universal offer of mercy, promise to overcome every man's aversion to believe and repent and his resistance of common grace. Election and preterition have no reference to the offer of salvation or to common grace. They relate only to special grace and the effectual application of Christ's sacrifice. The universal offer of mercy taught in this section evinces the universality of God's compassion towards sinners.

Larger Catechism, 63, declares that 'the ministry of the gospel testifies that whosoever believes in Christ shall be saved, and excludes none that will come unto him'. The reference here is not to the members of the visible Church, as one reviser contends who denies that the universal offer is in this section, because the persons spoken of are those

[27]

who have not yet believed in Christ, and have not yet come to him. The motive is held out to such persons, that if they *will* believe and come, they shall be saved by the infinite and universal mercy of God which 'excludes none that will come unto him'.

With what show of reason can it be said that a symbol containing such declarations as these respecting the nature and attributes of God, his requirement that every man confess sin to him, repent of it, pray for its forgiveness and trust in his mercy, contains no announcement of his infinite love and compassion? This great and blessed truth is worked and woven all through the Standards, as the doctrines of the Divine existence and the immortality of the soul are through the Bible. The Bible is nonsense without these latter, and the Confession is nonsense without the former.

The Westminster creed is being wounded in the house of its friends. To a spectator it appears amazing that so many who have 'received and accepted' it as teaching 'the system of doctrine contained in the Scriptures' should charge so many and so great errors upon it. If the Confession and Catechisms really are what they have been alleged to be, during the last six months, by some advocates of revision, they ought not to be revised at all, but to be repudiated.

5: *The Meaning and Value of the Doctrine of Decrees.*[1]

The proposal to revise the Westminster Standards has brought the doctrine of the Divine Decrees into the foreground. The controversy turns upon this pivot. Other features come in incidentally, but this is capital and controlling. This is the stone of stumbling and rock of offence. If election and reprobation were not in the Confession and Catechism, probably the fifteen presbyteries would not have overtured the Assembly. It is for this reason that we purpose to discuss the *Meaning and Value of the Doctrine of Decrees*, so plainly inculcated in the Scriptures, and from them introduced into the Westminster symbol. We are certain that the Biblical truth of the sovereignty of God in the salvation of sinners, and of his just liberty to determine how many he will save from their sin, and how many he will leave to their self-will in sin, is greatly misunderstood by some who profess the Presbyterian faith, and who describe it in much the same terms with the anti-Calvinist, and inveigh against it with something of the same bitterness. Though differing greatly from one another in personal feeling and attitude towards the Confession, the conservative and the radical reviser nevertheless practically meet together at this point, and while the former has no desire to make any

[1] By permission, from the Presbyterian and Reformed Review, January, 1890.

changes in the doctrine of decrees that will essentially impair the integrity of the Calvinistic system, he yet unintentionally aids the radical in bringing about a revolution in the sentiment and creed of the Presbyterian Church concerning one of the most distinctive articles of its belief. Because revision, be it conservative or radical, contends that *there is more or less that is un-scriptural* in the tenets of election and reprobation as they are now formulated in the Standards, and that they are bad in their influence. The amount of error in them, and the degree in which they are injurious, is variously stated by advocates of revision. But the general opinion of this class is, that they require more or less amending to get rid of certain elements that are derogatory to the character of God, and are inconsistent with the Christian redemption. Anti-revision denies this. The only question of importance, therefore, in this juncture, is: Revision, or Nonrevision. And this, as we have said, turns mainly upon the third chapter of the Confession, entitled 'Of God's Eternal Decree', together with the kindred declarations growing out of this, in other parts of the Standards. It will therefore be our aim to show that the doctrine of decrees, as it is found in the Westminster Standards, is neither un-scriptural nor erroneous; and that it is a highly useful and edifying doctrine in the formation of the Christian character. We heartily adopt the affirmation of the Thirty-nine Articles, that 'the godly consideration of predestination, and our election in Christ, is full of sweet, pleasant, and unspeakable comfort to godly persons, and such as feel in themselves the workings of the Spirit of Christ, mortifying the works of the flesh and their earthly members, and drawing up their minds to high and heavenly things, as well because it doth greatly establish and confirm their faith, and fervently kindle their love towards God'.

In carrying out our purpose, we shall mention certain characteristics of the Westminster doctrine that are both Scriptural and rational, and of great value both speculatively in constructing the Christian system, and practically in forming the Christian experience.

1. The first characteristic of the Confessional statement that we mention is, that it *brings sin within the scope, and under the control of the Divine decree.* Sin is one of the 'whatsoevers' that have 'come to pass', all of which are 'ordained'. Some would have the doctrine that sin is decreed stricken from the Confession, because in their view it makes God the author of sin. The Confession denies this in its assertion that by the Divine decree 'violence is not offered to the will of the creature, nor is the liberty of second causes taken away, but rather established'. In so saying, the authors had in mind the common distinction recognized in Calvinistic creeds and systems, between the efficient and the permissive decree, though they do not use the terms here. The latter, like the former, makes an event *certain*, but by a *different mode* from that of the former. When God executes his decree that Saul of Tarsus shall be 'a vessel of mercy', he works efficiently within him by his Holy Spirit 'to will and to do'. When God executes his decree that Judas Iscariot shall be 'a vessel of wrath fitted for destruction', he does not work efficiently within him 'to will and to do', but permissively in the way of allowing him to have his own wicked will. He decides not to restrain him or to regenerate him, but to leave him to his own obstinate and rebellious inclination and purpose; and accordingly 'the Son of man goeth, as it was determined, but woe unto that man by whom he is betrayed' (*Luke 22: 22; Acts 2: 23*). The two Divine methods in the two cases are plainly different, but the perdition of Judas was as much foreordained and free from chance, as the conversion of Saul. Man's inability to

explain how God can make sin certain, but not compulsory, by a *permissive* decree, is no reason for denying that he can do it or that he has done it. Appendix, Note 2.

It is sometimes argued that the Confession excludes the tenet of the permissive decree, by its declaration that the 'providence of God extendeth itself even to the first fall, and all other sins of angels and men, and that *not by a bare permission*' (*Conf. v. 4*). The 'bare permission' which the Assembly rejects here is that of the Tridentine theologians, who asserted that sin arises from the 'mere permission' of God. The Reformed theologians understood this to mean, that in respect to the fall of angels and men God is an idle and helpless spectator (deo otioso spectante), and that sin came into the universe without any positive *decision* and *purpose* on his part. This kind of 'permission' implies that God could not have *prevented* sin had he so decided, and is really no permission at all; because no one can properly be said to permit what he cannot prevent. In order to exclude this view of 'permission', the Assembly assert '*such* [a permission] as hath joined with it a most holy, wise, and powerful *bounding* and otherwise *ordering* and *governing* of [the sins of angels and men], in a manifold dispensation, to his own holy ends; *yet so as the sinfulness thereof proceedeth only from the creature, not from God, who neither is nor can be the author of sin*'. This last clause declares that God's relation to the sin which he decrees, is not that of efficiency, but permission. For if God worked directly and efficiently in angel or man 'to will', when he wills wickedly, the 'sinfulness of sin' would 'proceed from God', and God would be 'the author of sin'. The permissive decree is taught also in Larger Catechism, 19. 'God by his providence *permitted* some of the angels, wilfully and irrecoverably, to fall into sin and damnation, *limiting* and *ordering* that, and all their sins, to his own glory.'

The permissive decree is supported by Scripture, in the statement that God 'in times past suffered (εἴασε) all nations to walk in their own ways' (*Acts 14: 16*); that 'the times of this ignorance God overlooked' (ὑπεριδών) (*Acts 17: 30*); that God 'gave rebellious Israel their own desire' (*Psalm 78: 29*); that 'he gave them their request' (*Psalm 106: 15*). This phraseology is never employed when holiness is spoken of. The Bible never says that God *permits* man to be holy, or to act righteously. He efficiently influences and actuates him to this. Accordingly the other Reformed creeds, like the Westminster, mark the difference between God's relation to holiness and sin. The Second Helvetic, Ch. viii., says: 'Quotiescunque Deus aliquid mali in Scriptura facere dicitur atque videtur, non ideo dicitur, quod homo malum non faciat, sed quod Deus fieri *sinat* et *non prohibeat*, justo suo judicio, qui prohibere potuisset, si voluisset'. The Belgic Confession, Art. 13, asserts that God's 'power and goodness are so great and incomprehensible, that he orders and executes his work in the most excellent and just manner even when the devil and wicked men act unjustly. We are persuaded that he so restrains the devil and all our enemies that without his will and *permission* they cannot hurt us'. The Dort Canons, i. 15, teach that 'God, out of his sovereign, most just, and unchangeable good pleasure hath decreed to *leave* some men in the common misery into which they have wilfully plunged themselves, and not to bestow upon them saving faith and the grace of conversion, but *permitting* them in his just judgment to follow their own way, at last, for the declaration of his justice, to condemn and punish them for ever, not only on account of their unbelief, but also for all their other sins'.

And here is the place to notice the error of those who represent supralapsarianism as differing from infralapsarianism by referring sin to the *efficient* decree, thereby making God the author of it. Dr. Schaff, for example, asserts that 'Calvin carried the doctrine of the Divine decrees beyond the Augustinian infralapsarianism, which makes the fall of Adam the object of a permissive or passive decree, to the very verge of supralapsarianism, which traces even the first sin to an efficient or positive decree' (Creeds, i. 453). But both schemes alike refer sin to the permissive decree, and both alike deny that God is the author of sin. Supralapsarians like Beza and Gomar repel this charge, which anti-Calvinists made against both divisions of the Calvinists. Brandt, who was on the Arminian side, so understood Gomar. In describing the difference between Arminius and Gomar, he says of the latter: 'Gomarus maintained that it was appointed, by an eternal decree of God, who among mankind should be saved, and who should be damned. From whence it resulted that some men should be drawn to righteousness, and being drawn were preserved from falling; but that God *suffered* all the rest to remain in the common corruption of human nature, and in their own iniquities' (Reformation in the Low Countires, Book xviii.). Calvin, Inst. III xxii., says that 'man falls according to the appointment of Divine providence, but falls by his own fault'.[1] The difference between them relates to an

---

[1]Shedd: Dogmatic Theology, i. 409 (Note). A remark is in place here, upon the often cited 'decretum horribile' of Calvin. The Divine sovereignty in the salvation of sinners when properly viewed, inspires a solemn and religious *awe* before that Infinite Being who, in the language of Elihu, 'giveth not account of any of his matters' (Job 33: 13). This is the meaning of Calvin's 'decretum quidem horribile fateor' (Inst. III. xxiii. 7). Those who quote this in disparagement of the doctrine of predestination, suppose that he used 'horrible' in the modern vulgar sense of 'hateful' and 'repulsive', as when persons speak of a 'horrible stench', or an 'awful noise'. Of course he could not have intended to pour contempt upon what he believed to be a truth of revelation by employing the word in this popular and somewhat slangy signification. Calvin was a highly educated classical scholar, and his

altogether different point: namely, the order in which the decrees of election and reprobation stand to that of creation. The supralapsarian asserts that in the logical order of nature (not of time, for all the decrees are eternal), the decree to elect and reprobate certain men is before (supra) the decree to create them; the infralapsarian, that it is after (infra). The former contends that God *begins* by electing some men and reprobating others, and in order to execute these two decrees creates man and permits (not efficiently causes) the fall. The infralapsarian contends that God begins by creating man and permitting (not causing) the fall, and then out of this fallen and guilty race elects some to life, and leaves others to their voluntary sin and its just penalty. The supralapsarian order is liable to the charge that 'God creates some men in order to damn them', because creation follows from reprobation. The infralapsarian order is not liable to this charge, because creation does not follow from reprobation, but precedes it.[1] The Westminster Assembly, in common with the Calvinistic creeds previously made, adopted the infralapsarian order, though some theologians, like the

---

Latin is as accurate and elegant as any since the days of Cicero and Virgil. In the classical writers, 'horror' sometimes signifies awe and veneration. Lucretius, for example, describes the worship of the gods as originating in the 'mortalibus insitus *horror*' (De Natura, v. 1164). The feeling of reverential fear is expressed in Jacob's words, 'How *dreadful* is this place!' (Gen. 28: 17). In this sense of the word, the doctrine of predestination might be called 'a dreadful decree', without disparaging it in the least.

[1] The Arminian Remonstrants stated the difference between the two divisions of Calvinists as follows: 'Our opponents teach, First, that God, as some [i.e., supralapsarians] assert, has ordained by an eternal and irresistible decree some from among men, whom he does not consider as *created* much less as *fallen*, to eternal life, and some to everlasting perdition, without any regard to their obedience or disobedience, in order to exert both his justice and his mercy. Secondly, that God, as others [i.e., infralapsarians] teach, considers mankind not only as *created* but *fallen* in Adam, and consequently

elder Hodge, find a concession to the supralapsarians in some of their phraseology.

The doctrine of the permissive decree has great value in two respects: (*a*) In taking sin out of the sphere of chance. (*b*) In explaining the tenet of preterition, or 'foreordination to everlasting death'.

First, by the permissive decree, sin is brought within the Divine plan of the universe, and under the Divine control. Whatever is undecreed must be by hap-hazard and accident. If sin does not occur by the Divine purpose and permission, it occurs by chance. And if sin occurs by chance, the deity, as in the ancient pagan theologies, is limited and hampered by it. He is not 'God over all'. Dualism is introduced into the theory of the universe. Evil is an independent and uncontrollable principle. God governs only in part. Sin with all its effects is beyond his sway. This dualism God condemns as error, in his words to Cyrus by Isaiah, 'I make peace and create evil;' and in the words of Proverbs 16: 4, 'The Lord hath made all things for himself; yea, even the wicked for the day of evil'. 'We believe', says the Belgic Confession, Art. 13, 'that God after he had created all things did not forsake them, or give them up to fortune or chance, but that he rules and governs them according to his holy will, so that nothing happens in this world without his appointment; nevertheless, God neither is the author of, nor can be charged with, the sins which are committed'.

Secondly, by the permissive decree, the preterition of some sinners and thereby their 'foreordination to everlast-

---

as obnoxious to the curse; from which fall and destruction he has determined to release some, and save them as instances of his mercy, and to leave others under the curse for examples of his justice, without any regard to belief or unbelief' (Brandt: Reformation in the Low Countries, Book xix).

ing death' is shown to be rational as well as Scriptural, because God, while decreeing the destiny of the non-elect, is not the author of his sin or of his perdition. Preterition is a branch of the permissive decree, and stands or falls with it. Whoever would strike the doctrine of preterition from the Standards, to be consistent must strike out the general doctrine that sin is decreed. If God could permissively decree the fall of Adam and his posterity without being the cause and author of it, he can also permissively decree the eternal death of an individual sinner without being the cause and author of it. In preterition, God repeats, in respect to an individual, the act which he performed in respect to the race. He permitted the whole human species to fall in Adam in such a manner that they were responsible and guilty for the fall, and he permits an individual of the species to remain a sinner and to be lost by sin, in such a manner that the sinner is responsible and guilty for this.

The Westminster Standards, in common with the Calvinistic creeds generally, begin with affirming the universal sovereignty of God over his entire universe: over heaven, earth, and hell; and comprehend all beings and all events under his dominion. Nothing comes to pass contrary to his decree. Nothing happens by chance. Even moral evil, which he abhors and forbids, occurs by 'the determinate counsel and foreknowledge of God'; and yet occurs through the agency of the unforced and self-determining will of man as the efficient.

Why should such a tenet as this, taught by Scripture and supported by reason, be stricken out of the Confession; or if not stricken out, so minimized as to declare that God decrees holiness but not sin, elects but does not pass by? On the contrary, why should it not be proclaimed boldly and everywhere, that above all the sin, and the misery caused by sin, in this world of mankind, there sits on the throne a wise, benevolent, and omnipotent Sovereign who for reasons sufficient in his view *permitted*, but did not *cause* or *compel*, the fall of angels and men, with the intention of guiding the issue of it all to an ultimate end worthy of himself – namely, the manifestation of his two great attributes of mercy and justice: of mercy, in the salvation from sin of 'a great multitude whom no man can number'; of justice, in leaving a multitude that can be numbered to the sin which they love and prefer, and its righteous punishment.

2. The second characteristic of the Westminster doctrine of decrees is *the union of election and preterition*. It includes both tenets, and is consistent in doing so. The discontent with the Confession is greater upon this point than upon the first that we have mentioned. Many do not object to what the Standards say upon the abstract subject of the Divine decree, who particularly dislike its concrete teaching upon election and preterition. The discrimination which the Confession makes between sinners; the Divine purpose to save some and not all; they assert to be un-Biblical and unjust. 'The foreordination of some men to everlasting life, and of others to everlasting death, and preterition of all the non-elect, are equally inconsistent with a proper conception of Divine justice', is the assertion of a strenuous advocate of revision. Some would strike out both election and preterition; others would strike out preterition and retain election. We shall endeavor to show that one of these proposals is as destructive of the integrity of the system as the other; that both tenets must stand, or both must go.

That individual election is taught in the Bible is very generally conceded. But individual preterition is taught with equal plainness. The Lord Jesus Christ, the Saviour of sinners, is as explicit upon this subject as he is upon that of endless punishment. Upon two occasions (*Matt. 13: 14,*

15; John 12: 38–40), he quotes the words of God to Isaiah, 6: 9, 10: 'Go and tell this people, Hear ye indeed, but understand not; and see ye indeed, but perceive not. Make the heart of this people fat, and make their ears heavy, and shut their eyes; lest they see with their eyes, and hear with their ears, and understand with their heart, and convert, and be healed'. The prophet was instructed to declare the preterition of a part of Israel, and our Lord endorses the doctrine. And he frequently connects the voluntary and guilty rejection of his gracious offer of mercy with the eternal purpose and plan of God. The impenitence of Capernaum and of Chorazin and Bethsaida was guilty, and punishable with a punishment greater than that of Sodom; yet these sinners were 'the wise and prudent' from whom the 'Lord of heaven and earth' had 'hid the things' of salvation (*Matt. 11: 20–26*). 'Many', he says, 'are called, but few are chosen' (*Matt. 22: 14; Luke 17: 34–36*). With grief and tears over the hardness of heart and the bitter enmity of the Jerusalem sinners, he at the same time declares their reprobation by God. 'Upon you shall come all the righteous blood shed upon earth, from the blood of righteous Abel unto the blood of Zacharias. Behold, your house is left unto you desolate' (*Matt. 23: 35–38*). That the Apostolical Epistles teach preterition, we need not stop to prove. One principal objection made to the Pauline Christianity by its opponents is, that it is full of predestination both to holiness and sin. The Dort Canons, I. vi., enunciate Paul's doctrine in the following statement: 'That some receive the gift of faith from God, and others do not receive it, proceeds from God's eternal decree. According to which decree, he graciously softens the hearts of the elect, however obstinate, and inclines them to believe; while he leaves the non-elect in his just judgment to their own wickedness and obduracy'. 'Unto you', says our Lord, 'it is given to know the mysteries of

[39]

the kingdom of Heaven, but to them it is not given' (*Matt. 13: 11*).

Not only are both individual election and preterition taught in Scripture, but both are necessary in a creed in order to self-consistence. Preterition is the contrary of election, and one of two contraries necessarily implies the other. Right implies wrong; light implies darkness. No one would contend that there is light but not darkness; right but not wrong. And no one should contend that there is an election of individuals, but not a preterition.[1] It is impossible to think of individual election alone by itself, or to teach it alone by itself. Individual election implies and suggests individual reprobation. The elect himself (that is, one who hopes he is of the elect) sometimes fears that he is one of the non-elect. St. Paul kept his body under, lest he should be a reprobate 'cast away'. That Christian who denies the doctrine of preterition, and does not sometimes fear that God may pass him by, is not a model for imperfectly sanctified men. If God does not elect a sinner, he must of course pass him by. If God decides not to convert a sinner into a saint, he must of course decide to let him remain a sinner. If God does not purpose to make Judas Iscariot 'a vessel of mercy', he must of course purpose to leave him 'a vessel of wrath'. Individual election without its antithetic preterition is

[1] The qualifying epithet 'individual' is important here; because while *individual* election implies individual preterition as its contrary, *classical* election does not. If a whole class (say dying infants) are elected, no individuals of it are passed by. The true contrary to *classical* election is *classical* preterition, not individual preterition. In classical election, there cannot be the salvation of a part and perdition of a part, as there can be in individual election. The whole class must either be elected, or else the whole class must be passed by; the whole of it must be the objects of mercy, or else the whole of it must be the objects of justice. All must be saved, or else all must be lost. No discrimination is possible between individuals, as is the case in individual election.

only one-half of the circle of Divine truth. When God operates efficiently in the sinner's heart, to overcome his resistance of common grace, and his enmity to the law of God, this is election. When God does not work efficiently, but permissively leaves the sinner to himself, this is preterition. And he must do one thing or the other, in the instance of every sinner. And he must purpose to do one thing or the other, in every instance. And the purpose is an eternal one. Consequently to affirm in a creed the decree of individual election, and deny that of preterition, is the height of absurdity.

Accordingly, the Reformed creeds contain both doctrines; sometimes both of them verbally expressed, and sometimes preterition implied from election verbally expressed. Both doctrines are specified in the following symbols: Second Helvetic, Gallican, Belgic, First Scotch, Irish, Lambeth, Dort, Westminster. Election alone is specified in Augsburg, First Helvetic, Heidelberg, and Thirty-nine Articles. That the decree of individual election necessarily involves the antithetic decree of individual preterition, is evinced by the fact that Ursinus, one of the authors, and the principal one, of the Heidelberg Catechism, which verbally affirms election but not preterition, presents an elaborate statement and defence of reprobation in his Christian Theology (Qu. 54), composed in explanation of this creed.[1]

[1]Dr. Schaff, in the Evangelist, for November 14, 1889, asserts that the Gallican, Belgic, Second Helvetic, First Scotch, and Dort symbols, 'are silent on the decree of reprobation and preterition'. The following extracts from his Creeds of Christendom show that this is an error. Gallican, Art. 12: 'God calleth out of corruption and condemnation those whom he hath chosen without consideration of their works, in order to display in them the riches of his mercy; *leaving* (laissant) the rest in this same corruption and condemnation, in order to manifest in them his justice'. Belgic, Art. 16: 'God is merciful, since he delivers from perdition all whom he hath elected in Christ Jesus, without any respect to their works; just, in *leaving* (laissant) the

What is preterition? It is God's passing by a sinner in the bestowment of *regenerating*, not of common grace. All men are blessed with common grace. There is no election or reprobation in this reference. God's mercy in *this* form and degree of it is universal and indiscriminate. But common grace fails to save the sinner, because of his love of sin, his aversion to holiness, and his unbelief. The martyr Stephen's words are applicable to every man in respect to common grace: 'Ye stiff-necked, ye do always resist the Holy Ghost' (*Acts 7: 51*). Consequently, in order to save any sinner whatsoever requires a still higher grade of grace which, in the phrase of the Larger Catechism (67), 'powerfully determines' his will by regenerating it. Here is where the Divine discrimination comes in. It is with reference to *this* kind and degree of grace that God says: 'I will have mercy on whom I will have mercy' (*Ex. 33: 19; Rom. 9: 15*). And this is the Scripture truth which is now on trial in the Presbyterian Church. This is the particular doctrine which excites animosity in some

---

others in the fall and perdition wherein they have precipitated themselves'. Second Helvetic, Cap. x. 4, 6: 'Though God knows who are his, and sometimes the fewness of the elect is spoken of, yet we are to have hope for all, and no one is rashly to be numbered with the *reprobate*. We do not approve of the impious words of those who say: "If I am elected, I shall be saved, however I may act; if I am one of the *reprobate*, neither faith nor repentance will be of any use, since the decree of God cannot be altered"'. First Scotch, Art. 8: 'For this cause we are not afraid to call God our Father, not so much because he has created us, which we have in common with the *reprobate*, as that he has given to us his only Son to be our brother.' Dort Canons, i. 15: 'Holy Scripture testifieth that not all, but some only, are elected, while others are passed by in the eternal decree; whom God out of his sovereign good pleasure hath decreed to *leave* in the misery into which they have wilfully plunged themselves, permitting them to follow their own way. And this is the doctrine of *reprobation*, which by no means makes God the author of sin (the very thought of which is blasphemy), but declares him to be a righteous judge and punisher of sin'.

minds, and which it is contended must be cut out of the Confession like cancerous matter that is killing the body. Let us consider the objections that are made to it.

1. It is objected that preterition is *inconsistent with the infinite compassion* of God for the souls of all men, and cannot be squared with such assertions as, 'As I live, saith the Lord, I have no pleasure in the death of the wicked; but that the wicked turn from his way and live: turn ye, turn ye, for why will ye die?' 'God so loved the world that he gave his only-begotten Son, that whosoever believeth in him might not perish but have everlasting life'.

The first reply to this is, that these and many similar affirmations of the Divine pity for the sinful soul and desire for its salvation, are written in the same inspired volume that contains such assertions as the following: 'Many shall seek to enter in and shall not be able.' 'He hath blinded their eyes and hardened their hearts, that they should not see with their eyes, and be converted, and I should heal them.' 'The Son of man goeth as it was determined; but woe unto that man by whom he is betrayed.' 'I will have mercy on whom I will have mercy, and I will have compassion on whom I will have compassion. So then it is not of him that willeth, nor of him that runneth, but of God that sheweth mercy. The children being not yet born, neither having done any good or evil, that the purpose of God according to election might stand, not of works, but of him that calleth, it was said, The elder shall serve the younger. The disobedient stumble at the word, whereunto also they were appointed'. Since both classes of passages come from God, *he* must perceive that they are consistent with each other whether man can or not. Both, then, must be accepted as eternal truth by an act of faith, by every one who believes in the inspiration of the Bible. They must be presumed to be self-consistent, whether it can be shown or not.

But, secondly, there are *degrees* of mercy. Because God does not show the highest degree of it to a particular sinner, it does not follow that he does not show him any at all. He may grant him the mercy of common grace, and when this is resisted and nullified by his hostile self-will and obstinate love of sin, he may decide not to bestow the mercy of special grace, and yet not be chargeable with destitution of love and compassion towards him.[1] Any degree of love is love; and any degree of compassion is compassion. To contend that the Divine love must be of exactly the same degree towards all creatures alike or else it is not love, is untenable. It is certain that God can feel love and pity towards the souls of all men, as his creatures and as sinners lost by their own fault, and manifest it in that measure of grace which 'leads to repentance' (*Rom. 2: 4*), and would result in it if it were not resisted, and yet not actually save them all from the consequences of their own action. The Scriptures plainly teach that God so loved the whole world that he gave his only-begotten Son to make expiation for 'the sins of the whole world'; and they just as plainly teach that a part of this world of mankind are sentenced, by God, to eternal death for their sins. The Arminian and the Calvinist both alike deny the doctrine of universal salvation, yet believe that this is compatible with the doctrine of God's universal benevolence. Both deny the inference that if God does not save every human being, he does not love the soul of every human being; that if he does not do as much for one person as he does for another, he is unmerciful towards him. It is a fallacy to maintain, that unless God does *all that he possibly can* to save a sinner, he does not do anything towards his salvation; as it would

[1] Man is compelled to speak of God's decision or decree in this way, though strictly there is no before or after for him. All his decrees are eternal and simultaneous. Yet there is an order of nature. Special grace supposes the failure of common grace.

[44]

be fallacious to maintain, that unless God bestows upon a person all the temporal blessings that are within his power, he does not show him any benevolence at all. This fallacy lies under the argument against preterition. It is asserted that if God 'passes by' a sinner in the bestowment of regenerating grace, he has no love for his soul, no desire for its salvation, and does nothing towards its welfare. But if God really felt no compassion for a sinner, and showed him none, he would immediately *punish him for his sin*, and the matter would end here. The sinner's doom would be fixed. Just retribution would follow transgression instantaneously, and for ever. And who can impeach justice? 'As all men have sinned in Adam, and are obnoxious to eternal death, God would have done no injustice by leaving them all to perish, and delivering them over to condemnation on account of sin, according to the words of the Apostle: "That every mouth may be stopped, and all the world may become guilty before God"' (*Dort Canons, I. i.*). But God does not do this. He suffers long and is forbearing with every sinner without exception. There is not a transgressor on earth, in Christendom or Heathendom, who is not treated by his Maker *better than he deserves*; who does not experience some degree of the Divine love and compassion. God showers down upon all men the blessings of his providence, and bestows upon them all more or less of the common influences and operation of the Holy Spirit. This is mercy to the souls of men universally, and ought to move them to repent of sin and forsake it. This common grace and universal benevolence of God is often spoken of in Scripture. 'Despisest thou, O man, the riches of God's goodness, and forbearance, and long-suffering, not knowing [recognizing] that the goodness of God leads [tends to lead] thee to repentance; but after thy hardness and impenitent heart treasurest up unto thyself wrath against the day of wrath?' (*Rom. 2: 4, 5*). Here is the

[45]

common grace of God enjoyed by men universally, and thwarted by their love of sin, and obstinate self-will in sin. But is God unmerciful and destitute of compassion towards this man, if he decides to proceed no further with him, but leave him where he is, and as he is? Is all that God has done for him in the way of long-suffering, forbearance, kindness, and inward monitions in his conscience, to count for nothing? If this treatment of the sinner is not benevolence and compassion, what is it? It is mercy in God to reveal to every man the law of God, nay even 'the wrath of God against all ungodliness and unrighteousness of men who hold the truth in unrighteousness', for by this revelation the man is warned and urged to turn from sin and live. This is one way in which God says to the sinner, 'Turn ye, turn ye, for why will ye die? As I live I have no pleasure in the death of him that dieth'. It is mercy in God, and is so represented by St. Paul, when he 'does not leave himself without witness, in that he does good, sending rain from heaven, and fruitful seasons, filling men's hearts with food and gladness, and makes of one blood all nations of men for to dwell on all the face of the earth, and determines the bounds of their habitation, that they should seek the Lord, if haply they might feel after him, and find him, though he be not far from every one of us' (*Acts 14: 17; 17: 26, 27*). That this gracious and fatherly interest in their souls' welfare is repelled and nullified by their preference for sin and love of worldly pleasure, and comes to naught, does not alter the nature of it as it lies in the heart of God. It is Divine mercy and love for human souls, notwithstanding its ill success.

Common grace is great and undeserved mercy to a sinner, and would save him if he did not resist and frustrate it. In and by it, 'God commandeth all men everywhere to repent', and whoever repents will find mercy. In and by it, God commands every hearer of the written word to believe on the Lord Jesus Christ, and whoever believes shall be saved. The common grace of God consists of the written, or in the instance of the heathen the unwritten word, together with more or less of the *convicting* operation of the Holy Spirit. Says Hodge (ii. 667), 'The Bible teaches that the Holy Spirit, as the Spirit of truth, of holiness, and of life in all its forms, is present with every human mind, enforcing truth, restraining from evil, exciting to good, and imparting wisdom, or strength, when, where, and in what measure seemeth to him good. In this sphere, also, he "divideth to every man severally as he will."' Whoever is in any degree convinced of sin, and is in any degree urged by his conscience to confess and forsake it, is a subject of common grace. And whoever stifles conviction, refuses confession, and 'holds down the truth in unrighteousness', resists common grace. St. Paul charges this sin upon both the heathen and the evangelized. Common grace, we repeat, is great and undeserved mercy to a sinner, and by it God evinces his pity for his soul, and his desire for its salvation. But man universally, unevangelized and evangelized, nullifies this form and degree of the Divine mercy, by his opposition. The opponent of preterition comes in here at this point, and contends that God is bound to go yet further than common grace with sinful man, and subdue his enmity by creating him anew in the spirit of his mind; and that if he 'passes him by', and leaves him where he is, and as he is, he has no love for his soul. The sovereignty of God in this matter of bestowing *regenerating* grace is denied. To bestow it upon Jacob but not upon Esau, upon some but not upon all, is said to be injustice and partiality.

Scripture denies that God is under obligation to follow up his defeated common grace with his irresistible special grace. It asserts his just liberty to do as he pleases in regard to imparting that measure of grace which produces the new birth, and makes the sinner 'willing in the day of God's power'. The passages have already been cited. And reason teaches the same truth. Mercy from its very nature is free and optional in its exercise. God may manifest great and unmerited compassion to all men in common grace and the outward call, and limit his compassion if he please to some men in special grace and the effectual call. He may call upon all men to repent and believe, and promise salvation to all that do so, and yet not *incline* all men to do so. No one will say that a man is insincere in offering a gift, if he does not along with it produce the disposition to accept it. And neither should one assert this of God. God sincerely desires that the sinner would hear his outward call, and that his common grace might succeed with him. He sincerely desires that everyone who hears the message: 'Ho, every one that thirsteth, come ye to the waters; yea, come, buy wine and milk without money', would come just as he is, and of his own free will, 'for all things are ready'. The fact that God does not go further than this with all men and conquer their aversion, is consistent with this desire. No one contends that God is not universally benevolent because he bestows *more* health, wealth, and intellect upon some than upon others. And no one should contend that he is not universally merciful, because he bestows *more* grace upon some than upon others. The omnipotence of God is able to save the whole world of mankind, and to our narrow vision it seems singular that he does not; but be this as it may, it is false to say that if he does not exert the *whole* of his power, he is an unmerciful being towards those who abuse his common grace. That degree of forbearance and long-suffering which God shows towards those who resist it, and that measure of effort which he puts forth to convert them, is real mercy towards their souls. It is the sinner who has thwarted this benevolent approach of God to his sinful heart. Millions of men in all ages are continually beating back God's mercy in the outward call and nullifying it. A man who has had common grace, has been the subject of the Divine compassion to this degree. If he resists it, he cannot charge God with unmercifulness, because he does not bestow upon him still greater mercy in the form of regenerating grace. A beggar who contemptuously rejects the five dollars offered by a benevolent man, cannot charge stinginess upon him because after this rejection of the five dollars he does not give him ten. Any sinner who complains of God's 'passing him by' in the bestowment of regenerating grace after his abuse of common grace, virtually says to the High and Holy One who inhabits eternity, 'Thou hast tried once to convert me from sin; now try again, and try harder'.[1]

God's desire that a sinner should 'turn and live' under common grace, is not incompatible with his purpose to leave him to 'eat of the fruit of his own ways, and be filled with his own devices' – which is the same thing as 'foreordaining him to everlasting death'. A decree of God may not be indicative of what he desires and loves. He decrees sin, but abhors and forbids it. He decrees the physical agony of millions of men in earthquake, flood,

[1] An advocate of revision remarks that 'the Calvinist is doubtless right in saying that God is under no obligations to save us. Still, even if this be the case, God may be, and I believe is under obligations to afford every man an opportunity to be saved; that he has no right to "pass by" anyone'. Two criticisms upon this suggest themselves. First, God in the outward call *does* afford every man an opportunity to be saved. To every evangelized man he says, 'Believe on the Lord Jesus Christ and thou shalt be saved'. This is 'an opportunity to be saved'. To every unevangelized man he says, 'Repent of thy sins, and I will forgive them'. This is 'an opportunity to be saved'. That in both instances the opportunity is rejected, does not destroy the fact. Secondly, if God is 'under obligations to afford the opportunity to be saved', then salvation is an act of justice and the performance of a duty. In affording man the opportunity to be saved, God discharges his obligations. In this case, 'grace is no more grace' (Rom. 9: 6).

and conflagration, but he does not take delight in it. His omnipotence could prevent this suffering in which he has no pleasure, but he decides for adequate reasons not to do so. Similarly he could prevent the eternal death of every single member of the human family, in which he takes no pleasure, but decides not to do so for reasons that are wise in his sight. The distinction between the revealed will and the secret will of God is a valid one;[1] and the latter of these wills may be no index of the former, but the exact contrary of it. This is particularly the case when evil is the thing decreed.[2]

2. Secondly, it is objected to preterition that it is *partiality*. It would be, if sinners had a claim upon God for his regenerating grace. In this case he could make no discrimination, and must regenerate and save all. Partiality is impossible within the sphere of mercy, because the conditions requisite to it are wanting. It can exist only within the sphere of justice, where there are *rights* and *duties; claims* and *obligations*. A debtor cannot pay some of his creditors and 'pass by' others, without partiality. But in the sphere of mercy, where there is no indebtedness, and no claim, the patron may give to one beggar and not to another, if he so please, because he 'may do what he will with his own' – that is, with what he does not owe to any one. The parable of the talents was spoken by our Lord to

---

[1] God's revealed will, or will of desire, is expressed in Isa. 55: 1; Ezek. 33: 11; 1 Tim. 2: 4; Tit. 2: 11. His secret will, or will of decision and purpose in particular instances, is expressed in Matt. 13: 11; John 6: 37, 44, 65; Rom. 9: 16, 18, 19.

[2] The difference between will as general desire and inclination, and will as a particular volition or decision in a special instance, is seen in human action and is well understood. For sufficient reasons, a man may decide in a particular case to do by a volition something entirely contrary to his uniform and abiding inclination. He is uniformly averse and disinclined to physical pain, but he may decide to have his leg amputated. This decision is his 'decree', and is no index of what he is pleased with.

illustrate the doctrine of the Divine sovereignty in the bestowment of *unmerited* gifts; and the regeneration of the soul is one of the greatest of them.

This is a conclusive answer to the charge of partiality and injustice, but some would avoid the charge by striking out the tenet of preterition, and retaining that of election. In this case, election becomes *universal*. If no men are omitted in the bestowment of regenerating grace, all men are elected. This is universal salvation, because all the elect are infallibly regenerated and saved. And this is the manner in which the Later Lutheranism handles the doctrine. It denies preterition, and strenuously opposes this article of the Reformed creed. If the Presbyterian Church, after having adopted preterition for two centuries, shall now declare that it is an un-Scriptural and erroneous tenet, the meaning of the revision will be, that God has no sovereign liberty to 'pass by' any sinners, but must save them all. This is the form in which election is held by Schleiermacher and his school. They contend that there is no reprobation of any sinner whatsoever. All men are elected, because to pass by any is injustice and partiality. 'Calling (vocatio)', says Dorner, 'is universal, for the Divine purpose of redemption is just as universal as the need and capacity of redemption so that *the notion of a Divine decree to pass by a portion of mankind, and to restore freedom of decision only to the rest*, is out of the question' (Christian Doctrine, iv. 183). It is this form of Universalism, which postulates the offer of mercy to all men as something due to them, if not in this life then in the next, and denies that the regenerating work of the Holy Spirit is confined to earth and time, but goes on in the intermediate state that is percolating into the Scotch and American Calvinism from the writings of one class of German divines. Should the presbyteries reject the doctrine of preterition they will help on this tendency. A creed like the Heidelberg, or the Thirty-nine Articles, may not have preterition verbally stated, and yet *imply* it by its statement of election and by other parts of the symbol. But if a creed like the Westminster, which has both doctrines verbally stated, is subsequently revised so as to *strike out* preterition, then this tenet cannot be implied. It is positively branded as error, and rejected by the revising Church. If therefore the presbyteries shall assert that God does not 'pass by' any sinner in respect to regenerating grace, they will commit themselves to universal salvation in the form above mentioned. Election will no longer be balanced and limited by preterition, but will be unlimited and universal.

And with this will be connected another fatal error: namely, that God is *under obligation* to elect and regenerate every man. If justice forbids him to 'pass by' any sinners, and 'ordain them to dishonor and wrath for their sin', he is bound to elect all sinners and 'predestinate them to everlasting life'. He has no liberty or sovereignty in the case. He cannot say, 'I will have mercy upon whom I will have mercy, and whom I will I harden [do not soften]' (*Rom. 9: 18*). This transmutes mercy into justice. Pardon becomes a Divine duty. The offer of Christ's sacrifice, nay even the providing of it, becomes a debt which God owes to every human creature. This is the assumption that lies under all the various modes of Universalism. Sinful men, loving sin, bent on sin, are told that they are entitled to the offer of mercy and regenerating grace; that they must have a 'fair opportunity' of salvation, if not here, then hereafter. Sinful men, full of self-indulgence, confessing no sin and putting up no prayer for forgiveness, and who have all their lifetime suppressed the monitions of conscience and quenched the Holy Spirit's strivings with them in his exercise of common grace, are taught that if God shall pass them by, and leave them to the sin that they prefer, he is an unmerciful despot.

And here is the point where the *practical value* of the doctrine of election and preterition is clearly seen. Without it, some of the indispensable characteristics of a genuine Christian experience are impossible. Hence it is that St. Paul continually employs it in producing true repentance for sin, deep humility before God, utter self-distrust, sole reliance on Christ's sacrifice, and a cheering hope and confidence of salvation, founded not on the sinner's ability and what God owes him, but on God's gracious and unobliged purpose and covenant. This is the doctrine which elicits from him the rapturous exclamation, 'O the depth of the riches both of the wisdom and knowledge of God. For who hath first given to him, and it shall be recompensed unto him again? For of him, and through him, and to him are all things: to whom be glory for ever. Amen'. This is the doctrine which instructs the believer to ascribe all his holy acts, even the act of faith itself, to the unmerited and sovereign grace of his redeeming God, and with Charles Wesley to sing:

Hangs my helpless soul on Thee.

It is said that the doctrine of preterition is not and cannot be preached. It does not require technical terms and syllogistical reasoning, in order to preach a doctrine. Who so preaches the doctrine of the Trinity, or of regeneration, or of original sin, or of vicarious atonement, or of endless punishment? The doctrine of preterition is preached whenever the herald proclaims to the transgressor of God's law that sin is guilt and not misfortune; that the criminal has no claim upon the pardoning power for pardon; that the Supreme Judge might justly inflict upon him the penalty which his sin deserves; that his soul is helplessly dependent upon the optional unobliged decision of his Maker and Saviour; and that it is nothing but God's special grace in regeneration that makes him to

[53]

differ from others who go down to perdition. That these humbling and searching truths are taught more thoroughly at some times than others, is true. That they will empty some pews at all times, is true. It may be that they are less taught now than formerly; and if so, this is not the time either to revise or construct creeds. But whenever the Divine Spirit is present with his illumination, and the Scriptures are plainly preached, they come into the foreground. If they shall be revised out of the Confession, it is certain that they will be taught less and less, and will finally disappear from the religious experience.

The sinner's acknowledgment that God might justly pass him by, and leave him in his resistance of common grace, is a necessary element in *genuine repentance*. Whoever denies this, lacks the broken and contrite heart. Such was the sorrow of the penitent thief: 'We are in this condemnation justly; for we receive the due reward of our deeds'. Such was the penitence of the prodigal son: 'Father, I have sinned against heaven, and am no more worthy to be called thy son; make me as one of thy hired servants'. Such was the temper of the leper: 'Lord, if thou wilt, thou canst make me clean'. No one of these penitents took the ground that God owed him pardon and regeneration, and that to pass him by and ordain him to the eternal death which sin deserves would be an act dishonorable to God. To deny God's sovereignty in his exercise of mercy, is to set up a claim for salvation, and whoever does this evinces that he has no true view of sin as ill desert, and no true sorrow for it as such. There is need of this doctrine in all ages, owing to the pride of the human heart, and its unwillingness to bend the knee and renounce all merit and confess all demerit before God. And there is special need of it in our age, when the Christian experience is defective at this point, and redemption is looked upon as something which God owes to mankind, and is bound to provide for them. Unless this important truth is repristinated, and restored to its proper place in the consciousness of the Church, the current of Restorationism will set stronger and stronger, and the result will be a great apostasy in Christendom. This is no time to eradicate it from the Calvinistic creeds, but on the contrary to reaffirm it with confidence, and defend it out of Scripture.

Some say that preterition is liable to be understood as *preventing* a sinner's salvation, and would have an explanation added to the doctrine, to the effect that this is not its meaning or intent. We would respect the opinion of any Christian believer who sincerely thinks that the language of the Standards is unguarded, and who does not desire to change their doctrines but only to make sure that they are understood. This is not revision, but *explanation*; and a declarative statement similar to that of the United Presbyterians, which leaves the Confession untouched, is the least objectionable of all the plans before the Presbyterian Churches. But if it be borne in mind that preterition is by the *permissive*, not efficient decree, what call is there for such a guarding clause? How does or can God's decision to leave a sinner to do just what he likes *hinder* the sinner from faith and repentance? How does or can God's purpose to save another sinner, prevent this sinner from smiting on his breast, saying, 'God, be merciful to me, a sinner?' 'It is not the fault of the gospel', say the Dort Canons (I., iii. iv. 9), 'nor of Christ offered therein, nor of God who calls men by the gospel and confers upon them various gifts, that those who are called by the ministry of the word refuse to come and be converted. The fault lies in themselves'. There is nothing *causative* in the decree of preterition. John Bunyan's statement of the matter is plain common sense. 'Eternal reprobation *makes* no man a sinner. The foreknowledge of God that the reprobate will perish, *makes* no man a sinner. God's infallible determining upon the damnation of him that perisheth, *makes* no man a sinner. God's patience and forbearance until the reprobate fits himself for eternal destruction, *makes* no man a sinner' (Reprobation Asserted, xi.). Whatever God does by a permissive decree, excludes causation on his part. God is not the author of the sin in which he *leaves* the sinner; or of the impenitence to which he *gives him over*. His action in preterition is inaction, rather than action. He decides to do nothing to prevent the free will of the sinner from its own action. With what color of reason can it be said that God *forces* a man into perdition, when this is all he does to him? that God *hinders* a man from faith and repentance, when he lets him entirely alone? To put the proposed explanation and caveat into the Confessional doctrine of preterition, would be like writing under Landseer's lions, 'These are not sheep', or under Paul Potter's bull, 'This is not a horse'.

The preterition of a sinner is not his *exclusion* from salvation. Exclusion is a positive act; but preterition is a negative one. When God gives special regenerating grace to only one of two persons, he does not work upon the other to prevent him from believing and repenting under the operation of the common grace which he has bestowed upon both alike. He merely leaves the other to his own free will to decide the matter; assuring him that if he repents he will forgive him; and if he believes he will save him. The bestowment of common grace upon the non-elect shows that non-election does not exclude from the kingdom of heaven by Divine efficiency, because common grace is not only an *incitation* to believe and repent, but an actual *help* towards it; and a help that is nullified solely by the resistance of the non-elect, and not by anything in the nature of common grace, or by any preventive action of God. The fault of the failure of common grace to save the sinner, is chargeable to the sinner alone; and he has no right to plead a fault of his own as the reason why he is entitled to special grace. It is absurd for him to contend that God has no right to refuse him regenerating grace, because he has defeated the Divine mercy in common grace. The true way out of the difficulty for the sinner is, not to demand regenerating grace as a debt by denying that God has the right to withhold it, but to confess the sinful abuse and frustration of common grace, and to cry with the leper: 'Lord, if thou wilt, thou canst make me clean'.

Having thus demonstrated the Scriptural and self-consistent character of the doctrine of decrees as contained in the Westminster Standards, we turn now to consider two erroneous conclusions that are drawn from it, which are urged as reasons for their revision: First, that it shuts out the entire heathen world from Christ's redemption; and, second, that it implies the damnation of a part of those who die in infancy.

Some advocates of revision seem, unintentionally probably, to load down the Confession with faults not belonging to it. They put the worst interpretation upon its terms and phraseology; insist that its defenders have no right to its necessary implications and natural inferences in determining what it really means; and that an analytic and positive affirmation of every particular point must be found in it. Interpreting in this prejudiced manner, they assert that the Standards do not declare the universal love and compassion of God; that they teach that God creates some men in order to damn them;[1] that their doctrine of

---

[1] A false exegesis of Romans 9: 20 is sometimes employed to prove that God *creates* men sinners. 'Shall the thing formed ($\pi\lambda\acute{\alpha}\sigma\mu\alpha$) say to him that formed ($\pi\lambda\acute{\alpha}\sigma\alpha\nu\tau\iota$) it, Why hast thou made me thus?' does not mean, 'Shall the thing *created* say to him that *created* it, Why hast thou *created* me thus?' Creation ex nihilo would require $\kappa\tau\acute{\iota}\sigma\iota\varsigma$, not $\pi\lambda\acute{\alpha}\sigma\mu\alpha$. The latter term denotes only the formative act of a moulder, not the supernatural act of a creator. The whole sinful mass of mankind whom God *created holy*, have become sinful by *their own* act, and lie in his hand like clay in the hands of the potter. Compare Isa. 29: 16; 45: 9. The potter, *as such*, does not give the clay

election discourages ministers from making the universal offer of Christ's salvation, and hinders sinners from accepting it; and that he who adopts them as they read cannot consistently believe that any of the heathen are saved, and that no dying infants are lost. They carry a wrong idea of election and reprobation into their exegesis of the Standards. They suppose that these necessarily imply that only a very few are elected, and that very many are reprobated. But there is nothing in the nature of either election or preterition, that determines the *number* of each; nothing that implies that the elect must be the minority, and the non-elect the majority, or the converse. The size of each circle depends upon the will of him who draws it. God, conceivably, might have elected the whole human family without an exception, as Schleiermacher says he did. Or, conceivably, he might have reprobated the whole human family, because he was not in justice obliged to save it. There is nothing in the nature of election that makes it inapplicable to the heathen, or of preterition. God may elect and regenerate a heathen if he please, or he may leave him in the sin which he loves. And the same is true of the ideas of election and preterition as related to dying infants. Since everything in this matter depends wholly upon the *sovereign will* of God, he may regulate his choice as he pleases. He may choose dying infants as individuals, as he does adults; or he may choose them as a class. And he might reject dying infants as individuals, as he does adults; or he might reject them as a class. For since infants like adults have a sinful nature, and, in the phrase of the Auburn Declaration, 'in order to

its properties, but merely shapes the clay into vessels of honor or dishonor as he pleases. Says Hodge, in loco, 'It is to be borne in mind, that Paul does not here speak of the right of God over his creatures as *creatures*, but as *sinful* creatures'. Compare Shedd: On Romans, 9: 20.

be saved, need redemption by the blood of Christ, and regeneration by the Holy Ghost', they require the exercise of *unmerited* mercy, which on grounds of justice might be withheld.

We cannot, therefore, determine from the mere idea of election how many are elected, or from that of preterition how many are passed by. This question can be answered only by God himself, and this answer, so far as he has vouchsafed to give it, is contained in his word. That the Scriptures plainly teach that the total result of Christ's redemption will be a triumphant victory over the kingdom of Satan, and that the number of the redeemed will be vastly greater than that of the lost, we shall assume. It is also plainly taught in Scripture, that God's *ordinary* method is to gather his elect from the evangelized part of mankind. Does Scripture also furnish ground for the belief, that God also gathers some of his elect by an *extraordinary* method from among the unevangelized, and without the written word saves some adult heathen 'by the washing of regeneration and renewing of the Holy Ghost'? We contend that the Confession so understands the Scriptures, in its declaration that there are some 'elect persons [other than infants] who are incapable of being outwardly called by the ministry of the word'. To refer the 'incapacity' here spoken of to that of idiots and insane persons, is an example of the unnatural exegesis of the Standards to which we have alluded. The hypothesis that the Confession teaches that there are elect and non-elect *idiots*, and elect and non-elect *maniacs*, is remarkable. It is incredible for two reasons. First, idiots and maniacs are not moral agents, and therefore as such are neither damnable nor salvable. They would be required to be made rational and sane, before they could be classed with the rest of mankind. It is utterly improbable that the Assembly took into account this very small number of individuals respecting whose destiny so little is known. It would be like taking into account abortions and untimely births. Secondly, these 'elect persons who are incapable of being outwardly called by the ministry of the word,' are contrasted in the immediate context with 'others not elected, who although they may be called by the ministry of the word never truly come to Christ'; that is to say, they are contrasted with rational and sane adults in evangelized regions. But idiots and maniacs could not be put into such a contrast. The 'incapacity' therefore must be that of circumstances, not of mental faculty. A man in the heart of unevangelized Africa is incapable of hearing the written word, in the sense that a man in New York is incapable of hearing the roar of London.

Consequently, the Confession, in this section, intends to teach that there are some unevangelized men who are 'regenerated and saved by Christ through the Spirit' without 'the ministry of the written word', and who differ in this respect from evangelized men who are regenerated in connection with it. There are these two classes of regenerated persons among God's elect. They are both alike in being born, 'not of blood, nor of the will of the flesh, nor of the will of man, but of God'. They are both alike in respect to faith and repentance, because these are the natural and necessary effects of regeneration. Both alike feel and confess sin; and both alike hope in the Divine mercy, though the regenerate heathen has not yet had Christ presented to him. As this is the extraordinary work of the Holy Spirit, little is said bearing upon it in Scripture. But something is said. God's promise to Abraham was, that in him should 'all the families of the earth be blessed' (*Gen. 12: 3*). St. Paul teaches that 'they are not all Israel which are of Israel' (*Rom. 9: 6*); and that 'they which are of faith, the same are the children of Abraham' (*Gal. 3: 7*). Our Lord affirms that 'many shall come from the east and west, the north and the south, and shall sit down with Abraham, and Isaac, and Jacob, in the kingdom of heaven' (*Matt. 8: 11*). Christ saw both penitence and faith in the unevangelized centurion, respecting whom he said, 'I have not found so great faith, no, not in Israel' (*Matt. 8: 5–10*). The faith of the 'woman of Canaan', an alien and stranger to the Jewish people and covenant, was tested more severely than that of any person who came to him in the days of his flesh, and of it the gracious Redeemer exclaimed, 'O woman, great is thy faith!'. These two classes of the regenerate have their typical heads in Scripture. Says Kurtz, 'Of those who are blessed in the seed of Abraham, Naomi represents the people of God who are to proceed from the ancient people of the covenant, and Ruth represents those proceeding from the heathen world'. That the Church is not to expect and rely upon this extraordinary work of the Spirit, it is needless to say. That this work is extensive, and the number of saved unevangelized adults is great, cannot be affirmed. But that all the adult heathen are lost is not the teaching of the Bible or of the Westminster Standards.

The declaration in Confession x. 4, and Larger Catechism, 60, does not refer at all to the heathen as such, but only to a certain class of persons to be found both in Christendom and heathendom, and probably more numerously in the former than in the latter. The 'men not professing the Christian religion' are those who *reject* it, either in spirit, or formally and actually; that is to say, *legalists* of every age and nation, evangelized or unevangelized, who expect future happiness by following 'the light of nature' and reason, and the ethical 'religion they do profess', instead of by confessing sin and hoping in the Divine mercy. The Jewish Pharisee, the Roman Julian and Antoninus, the self-satisfied Buddhist sage following the 'light of Asia', the Mohammedan saint despising Christianity, the English Hume and Mill, all of every race and clime who pride themselves on personal character and morality, and lack the humility and penitence that welcome the gospel, are the class spoken of in these declarations. They press no more, and probably less, upon the heathen than upon the Christian world; because the most hostile and intense rejection of the doctrines of grace is to be found in Christian countries, rather than in Pagan. They do not shut out of the kingdom of heaven any heathen who has the spirit of the publican, but do shut out every heathen and every nominal Christian who is destitute of it. The object of this section of the Confession, which is the same as the eighteenth of the Thirty-nine Articles, is to teach that no human creature, evangelized or unevangelized, can be saved on any but *evangelical* principles; namely, by unmerited grace, not by personal merit. It is only another way of proclaiming St. Paul's doctrine, that 'by the works of the law no flesh shall be justified'.

That this is the correct understanding of the Westminster Standards is corroborated by the fact that the Calvinism of the time held that God has his elect among the heathen. The Second Helvetic Confession (i. 7), teaches it. Zanchius, whose treatise on Predestination is of the strictest type, asserts it. Witsius and others suggest that the grace of God in election is wide and far reaching. The elder Calvinists held with the strictest rigor that no man is saved outside of the circle of election and regeneration, but they did not make that circle to be the small, narrow, insignificant circumference which their opponents charge upon them. And there is no reason to believe that the Westminster Assembly differed from the Calvinism of the time.

And this brings us to the subject of 'elect infants'. There

is no dispute that the Confession teaches that there are 'elect dying infants'. Does it also teach that there are 'non-elect dying infants?' In other words, does the phrase 'elect infants' imply that there are 'non-elect infants', as the phrase 'elect adults' does that there are 'non-elect adults'? This depends upon whether the cases are alike in all particulars. The argument is from analogy, and analogical reasoning requires a resemblance and similarity upon which to rest. But the Confession directs attention to a *great and marked diversity* between infant and adult regeneration, which sets off the two classes from one another, making some things true of one that are not of the other. The Confession points at and signalizes the striking difference in *the manner in which the Holy Ghost operates*, in each instance. Infants are incapable of the outward call and common grace; adults are capable of both. Consequently an elect infant dying in infancy is 'regenerated by Christ, through the Spirit', without the outward call and common grace; but an elect adult is 'regenerated by Christ through the Spirit', in connection with the external call and common grace, and after both have been frustrated by him. Election and non-election in the case of adults is the selection of some and omission of others who are alike guilty of resisting the ordinary antecedents of regeneration. Election in the case of dying infants is wholly apart from this. There being this great *dissimilarity* between the two classes, it does not follow that every particular that is true of one must be of the other; that because election is individual in the instance of adults it must necessarily be so in that of infants; that because adults are not elected as a *class* infants cannot be. The state of things in which the regeneration of an adult occurs, namely, after conviction of sin and more or less opposition to the truth, is entirely diverse from that in which the regeneration of a dying infant occurs; namely, in unconsciousness and without

[63]

conviction of sin. The only form of grace that is possible to the dying infant is regenerating grace, and the only call possible is the effectual call. If therefore God manifests any grace at all to the dying infant, it must be special and saving; and if he call him at all, he must call him effectually.

Now, since the authors of the Confession have themselves distinctly specified such a peculiar feature in the regeneration of the dying infant, it is plain that they regarded it as differing in some respects from that of adults, and intended to disconnect it from that of adults and consider it by itself. For why should they take pains, when speaking of elect infants, to call attention to the fact that the 'Holy Ghost worketh when, and where, and *how* he pleaseth', if they did not mean to signalize the *extraordinariness* of the Divine action in infant regeneration? And if infant regeneration is extraordinary in not having been preceded by the usual antecedents of common grace and the outward call, why may it not be extraordinary in being universal and not particular? that of a class and not of individuals? Does not the singularity that distinguishes the infant in regard to regeneration without conviction of sin, suggest that of electing the whole class? But what is far more conclusive, does not the fact that the Assembly *does not limit* infant election by infant preterition, as it limits adult election by adult preterition, actually prove that there is this great diversity in the two cases? Does not the fact that the Assembly, while explicitly, and with a carefulness that is irritating to many persons, balancing and guarding the election of adults by preterition, *does not do so* with the election of infants, show beyond doubt that they believed their election to be unlimited, and that no dying infants are 'passed by' in the bestowment of regenerating grace? We have already seen that the *proposed* omission of preterition, so as to leave only election in the case of adults, would make their election universal, and save the whole class without exception. The *actual* omission of it by the Assembly in the case of dying infants has the same effect. It is morally certain that if the Assembly had intended to discriminate between elect and non-elect infants, as they do between elect and non-elect adults, they would have taken pains to do so, and would have inserted a corresponding clause concerning infant preterition to indicate it. Whoever contends that they believed that preterition applies to infants, is bound to explain their silence upon this point. Had infant election been explicitly limited by infant preterition in the Confession, it would have been impossible for any candid expounder of it to hold that it permits subscribers to it to believe in the salvation of *all* dying infants. But Calvinistic divines for the last century or more have put this interpretation upon this section of the Confession, namely, that infant election is not individual but classical, and we think they are justified in so doing by the remarkable omission in this case.[1]

On the face of it, the thing looks probable. The case of the adult, in which there is both the outward call and the effectual, both common grace and regenerating, may be governed by the principle of individuality; while that of the infant, in which there is only the effectual call and regenerating grace, may be governed by the principle of community. Of those who have had the outward call and have rejected it, some may be taken and others left; while of those who have not had the outward call and have not

---

[1]Respecting the necessity of construing the Confession as teaching that there are non-elect infants, Dr. Schaff remarks as follows: 'The Confession nowhere speaks of reprobate infants, and the existence of such is not *necessarily* implied by way of distinction, although it *probably* was in the minds of the framers, as their private opinion, which they wisely withheld from the Confession' (Creeds of Christendom, i. 795).

rejected it, all may be taken. It is *election* in both instances; that is, the decision of God according to the counsel of his own will. In one case, God sovereignly decides to elect some; in the other, to elect all. And it is *unmerited mercy*, in both instances; because God is not bound and obliged by justice to pardon and eradicate the sin of an infant any more than that of an adult. And there is nothing in the fact that an infant has not resisted common grace, that *entitles* it to the exercise of special grace. In the transaction, God is moved wholly by his spontaneous and infinite mercy. He does an act to which he is not *compelled* by the sense of duty or of justice, either to himself or to sinners, but which he *loves* to do, and *longs* to do, because of his infinite pity and compassion.[1]

That many of the elder Calvinists believed that there are some non-elect infants is undeniable; and that in the long and heated discussions of the seventeenth century between Calvinists and Arminians, and between Calvinists themselves, many hard sayings were uttered by individual theologians which may be construed to prove that man is necessitated to sin, that God is the author of sin, and that the majority of mankind are lost, is equally undeniable. But the Westminster Confession must be held responsible for only what is declared on its pages. The question is not, whether few or many of the members of the Assembly held that some dying infants are lost, but whether the Confession so asserts; is not, whether any Calvinists of that day, in endeavoring to show *how* God decrees sin, may not have come perilously near representing him as

[1]The assumption that God is obliged by justice to offer salvation to all mankind, and to redeem them all, precludes all gratitude and praise for redemption, on their part. Why should they give thanks for a favor that is due to them, and which it is the duty of God to bestow? Christians adore 'the riches of God's grace' because it is utterly unclaimable on their part, and unobligated on his.

doing it by direct efficiency, but whether the Reformed and Westminster creeds do this.

The rigor of the theology of the elder Calvinists has been exaggerated. They took a wide and large view of the *possible extent* of election. Owen is as strict as most of them. But in arguing against the Arminians, in support of the guilt and condemnability of original sin, he says: 'Observe that in this inquiry of the desert of original sin, the question is not, *What shall be the certain lot of those who depart this life under the guilt of this sin only?* but, What this hereditary and native corruption doth *deserve*, in all those in whom it is? For as St. Paul saith, 'We judge not them that are without' (especially *infants*), I Cor. 5: 13. But for the *demerit* of it in the justice of God, our Saviour expressly affirmeth that 'unless a man be born again, he cannot enter into the kingdom of God'. Again, we are assured that no unclean thing shall enter into heaven (*Rev. 21*). Children are polluted with hell-deserving uncleanness, and therefore unless it be purged with the blood of Christ, they have no interest in everlasting happiness. By this means sin is come upon all to condemnation, and yet we do not peremptorily censure to hell *all infants departing out of this world without the laver of regeneration* [*i.e.*, baptism], the ordinary means of waiving the punishment due to this pollution. That is the question de facto, which we before rejected: yea, and *two* ways there are whereby God saveth such infants, snatching them like brands out of the fire. First, by interesting them in the covenant, if their immediate or remote parents have been believers. He is a God of them, and of their seed, extending his mercy unto a thousand generations of them that fear him. Secondly, by his grace of election, which is *most free* and *not tied to any conditions*; by which I make no doubt but God taketh many unto him in Christ *whose parents never knew, or had been despisers of the gospel*. And this is the doctrine of our

[67]

Church, agreeable to the Scripture, affirming the desert of original sin to be God's wrath and damnation' (Owen: Arminianism, Ch. vii.).[1] This is the salvation of infants by both covenanted and uncovenanted mercy, and Owen maintains that it is a tenet of Calvinism. That he does not assert the classical election of infants is true; but he asserts the individual election of some infants outside of the Church.

Such, then, is the Westminster doctrine of the Divine Decree. It is the common Augustino-Calvinistic doctrine. No part of it can be spared, and retain the integrity of the system. Whatever may have been the intention of the few first proposers of revision; or whatever may be the intention of the many various advocates of it who have joined them; the grave question before all parties now is, Whether the Presbyterian Church shall adhere to the historical Calvinism with which all its past usefulness and honor are inseparably associated, or whether it shall renounce it as an antiquated system which did good service in its day, but can do so no longer. The votes of the presbyteries within the coming six months will answer this question.

[1] Owen's Works vol. 10 p. 81.

6: *Preterition Necessary to the Sovereignty of God in Election*[1]

It is generally conceded by those who advocate a revision of the Confession, that 'the sovereignty of God in election' must be retained as a fundamental truth. Several presbyteries have voted for revision, with the explicit declaration that this part of the third chapter must stand; and they have at the same time voted to strike out the doctrine of *preterition*. Among them is the large and influential presbytery of New York. With the highest respect for our brethren and co-presbyters, and with sincere regret to be obliged to differ from the majority, we proceed to raise and answer the question, Whether the doctrine of 'the sovereignty of God in election' can be held unimpaired and in its integrity, if the tenet of preterition is omitted from 'the system of doctrine contained in the Scriptures'.

The presbytery have declared to the General Assembly: 1, That 'they deprecate most earnestly all such changes as would impair the essential articles of our faith'; and 2, That 'they desire the third chapter of the Confession, after the first section, to be so recast as to include these things only: The sovereignty of God in election; the general love of God for all mankind; the salvation in Christ Jesus provided for all, and to be preached to every creature'. In this recasting, they specify several sections of chapter

[1]New York Observer, March 6, 1890.

[69]

three which they would strike out, and among them is the section which declares that God 'passes by' some of mankind, and 'ordains them to dishonor and wrath for their sin'. According to this deliverance, the presbytery of New York supposes that it can hold the doctrine of 'the sovereignty of God in election' unimpaired and in all its essential features, while denying and rejecting the doctrine of preterition. An examination of the nature and definition of 'sovereignty', we think, will show that this is impossible.

Sovereignty is a comprehensive term. It contains several elements. First it denotes *supremacy*. A sovereign ruler is supreme in his dominions. All other rulers are under him. Secondly, sovereignty denotes *independence*. Says Woolsey, 'In the intercourse of nations certain states have a position of entire independence of others. They have the power of self-government, that is, of independence of all other states as far as their own territory and citizens are concerned. This power of independent action in external and internal relations constitutes complete sovereignty' (Political Science, i. 204). Thirdly, sovereignty denotes *optional power*; that is, the power to act or not in a given instance. It is more particularly with reference to this latter characteristic of free alternative decision, that 'the sovereignty of God in election' is spoken of. In his election of a sinner to salvation, God as supreme, independent, and sovereign, acts with entire liberty of decision, and not as obliged and shut up to one course of action.

This is the common understanding and definition of sovereignty as applied to decisions and acts. Says Blackstone: 'By the sovereign power is meant the power of making laws; for wherever that power resides all other powers must conform to, and be directed by it, whatever appearance the outward form and administration of the government may put on. For it is at any time in the *option* of the legislature to alter that form and administration by a new edict or rule, and put the execution of the law into whatever hands it pleases, by constituting one, or a few, or many executive magistrates' (Introduction, 2). Blackstone gives the same definition of sovereignty, when it is vested in a king (Book II., ch. vii.). The king has no superior to oblige or compel him to one course of action. He has independent and optional power. This is the reason why a monarchy is inferior to a republic, as an ideal of government, and the secret of the steady tendency to the latter form of government, in the earth. Sovereign, supreme, independent, and *optional* power is too great a power to be lodged in the hands of one man. Its safest deposit is in the hands of all the people.

The pardoning power is a sovereign power, and this implies choice between two alternatives. If the governor of New York has the power to grant a pardon to a criminal, but not the power to refuse it, he is not sovereign in the matter. If of two criminals, he cannot pardon one and leave the other under the sentence of the court, he is not sovereign in the matter. When it is said that in a democracy the sovereign power is vested in the people, the meaning is that the people have the right to make such a constitution and laws as they please. No one would contend that the people of New York have sovereign power in the case, if they are obliged to put imprisonment for debt, or any other particular statute, into their code. A 'sovereignty' that has no alternative is none at all.

God is a sovereign, and the highest of all. He may create a universe or not, as he pleases. Were he obliged or compelled to create, he would not be sovereign in creating. He may arrange and order his universe as he pleases. If he were confined to but one order, he would not be sovereign in his providence. But not to waste time on these self-evident generalities, we come to the case in hand: the 'sovereignty of God in *election*'. The question is, Whether God is 'sovereign' in electing, regenerating, and saving a sinner, if he has no *option* in the matter? if he cannot 'pass by' the sinner, and leave him unregenerate, unpardoned, and unsaved? One would think that such a question as this could have but one answer in the negative, had not a majority of the presbytery of New York answered it in the affirmative. The Westminster Confession declares that 'the sovereignty of God in election' means, that he may elect or pass by the sinner as he pleases. The Revised Confession declares that it means, that he may elect him but not pass him by. The Old Confession declares that sovereignty means, that God may bestow regenerating grace upon a sinner who is resisting common grace, or may not bestow it. The New Confession declares that it means, that he may bestow regenerating grace upon him, but may not refuse to bestow it. The Old Confession declares that sovereignty means, that God may pardon the sinner or not, as he pleases. The New Confession declares that it means, that he may pardon him but not deny him a pardon.

Now we ask, What *sovereignty* has God in the salvation of the sinner, if he has no alternative in regard to election, regeneration, and pardon? if eternal justice requires that he elect, and forbids that he pass by? if eternal justice requires that he regenerate, and forbids him to leave in unregeneracy? if eternal justice requires that he pardon, and forbids him to refuse to pardon? To strike out preterition from the Confession, is to declare that it is an unscriptural doctrine, and to brand it as error. And to assert 'the sovereignty of God in election' after having done this, is to assert that an act that has no alternative is a sovereign act.

But God himself has decided the question. He asserts his sovereign right to optional decision in the matter of human salvation. In that wonderful description of his being and attributes which he gave to Moses, among other declarations he says, 'I will be gracious to whom I will be gracious, and will shew mercy to whom I will shew mercy' (*Ex. 33: 19*). In this solemn pronunciamento with which he prefaced the whole work of human salvation, he distinctly declares that he is under no obligation to redeem sinful men, but that whatever he does in the premises is of his own unobliged, free, and sovereign mercy and decision. Still more explicitly, in what is perhaps the most terrible passage in all Scripture, God asserts that he will pass by and leave in their sin some who have refused his common call, and frustrated his common grace. 'Because I have called, and ye refused; I have stretched out my hand, and no man regarded; but ye have set at nought all my counsel, and would none of my reproof; I also will laugh at your calamity; I will mock when your fear cometh. Then shall they call upon me, but I will not answer; they shall seek me early, but they shall not find me' (*Prov. 1: 24–26, 27*). God incarnate teaches the same truth, that 'one shall be taken and the other left' (*Luke 17: 34-36*) And St. Paul recites the words of God to Moses, 'I will have mercy on whom I will have mercy, and I will have compassion on whom I will have compassion', as a conclusive demonstration of the Divine sovereignty in salvation.

The only instance of the retention of election, and rejection of preterition, in a creed, is that of the Cumberland Presbyterians. Our Arminian brethren are consistent and logical, like the Westminster Standards, in teaching both election and preterition; only they assert that both are conditional. Men are elected because of faith, and are passed by because of unbelief. There has never been any proposition to revise preterition out of an Arminian creed. Arminius, Episcopius, Limborch, Wesley, and Watson understand that election necessarily implies the antithetic non-election.[1] A proposition to revise the Confession so that it would teach *conditional* election and preterition, would be self-consistent but anti-Calvinistic; but the proposition to revise it so as to declare that God elects but does not pass by sinners, is neither consistency nor Calvinism. If adopted, the Northern Presbyterian Church will have an illegal and mutilated creed, and will resemble a wounded eagle attempting to fly with but one wing.

[1]According to Brandt, the Remonstrants defined predestination as follows: 'God hath decreed from all eternity to elect those to everlasting life, who through his grace believe in Jesus Christ and persevere in faith and obedience; and on the contrary hath resolved to *reject* the unconverted and unbelieving to everlasting damnation' (Reformation in the Low Countries, Book xxi.).

7: *Preterition and the Lopsided View of the Divine Decree*

The doctrine of the Divine decree is inseparably connected with that of the manifestation of the Divine glory, because the latter is the end and aim of the former. Some Presbyteries recommend a one-sided fractional view of the Divine decree, by striking out reprobation from the Westminster Confession and leaving election as it now stands. In order to determine whether this view of the divine decree is Scriptural or rational, it is necessary to determine what is meant by the manifestation of the Divine glory, and whether it can be secured by manifesting only the mercy of God to the exclusion of his justice.

The 'glory of God' means either his essential or his manifested glory. It is the manifested glory that is intended when the question is asked, whether God does everything for his own glory; whether in all his works his object is to reveal to angels and men the intrinsic and inherent glory of his being and nature. One would say, on the face of it, that this is no question at all. What else should God do anything for, but to show that he is an infinitely perfect and good being? but to exhibit in various ways his natural and moral qualities?

1. The essential glory of God means all that is glorious in God. In the Scriptures 'glory' is a general term to denote the sum-total of all the qualities that constitute the Divine excellence. The nature and attributes of God are the glory

of God. They make him a glorious being. In this sense the 'glory of God' is only another name for infinite perfection; only another name for the entire aggregate of the Divine attributes. Sometimes the phrase has chief reference to God's natural attributes, as seen in the material universe. 'The heavens declare the glory of God'. 'O Lord, our Lord, how excellent is thy name in all the earth! who hast set thy glory above [or upon] the heavens'. Such texts as these speak of the glory, or glorious excellence, of God as displayed in creation and providence. Sometimes the principal reference is to God's moral attributes, as seen in redemption. 'I will send those that escape from them unto the nations, and they shall declare my glory among the Gentiles'. 'Declare his glory among the heathen'. In Eph. 1: 14, 'The redemption of the purchased possession is unto the praise of God's glory'. In Phil. 1: 11, 'The fruits of righteousness which are by Jesus Christ are unto the glory and praise of God'. Such scriptures as these show that the 'glory of God' does not mean self-applause but moral excellence; and that when God is said to do all things for his own glory, the meaning is that he does them for the purpose of revealing in nature and grace his infinite perfections. When therefore the phrase is defined in accordance with its use in the Bible, and with the idea of an infinitely perfect being, it has nothing that should excite opposition. There is not the slightest reason for confounding it with human vanity, or the selfish love of fame among men.

The essential glory of God is a fixed quantity. There can be neither increase nor diminution of it. When man is commanded, 'whether he eat or drink, or whatever he does, to do all to the glory of God', it is not meant that his action can add anything to the inherent glory of God, and make him more glorious intrinsically than he was before. In respect to the essential glory of God, neither angel nor man can do anything. But the intrinsic and immutable excellence of God is capable of being manifested to angels and men, and also, in a secondary manner, by angels and men; for when angels and men recognize and acknowledge the glory of God by their acts of obedience and adoration, they too declare and set it forth in an inferior degree.

2. Secondly, the essential glory of God is the foundation of all worship. It is because the Supreme Being has this constellation of attributes, this sum-total of infinite perfections which is grouped under the name of 'glory', that he is worthy of adoration. If a single one of these attributes were wanting, the Divine glory would be defective; and a defective Being would not be worthy of the hallelujahs of heaven. Those who deny, either theoretically or practically, the Divine holiness and justice, and affirm only the Divine benevolence and mercy, mutilate the Divine nature and destroy the Divine glory. They metamorphose the Supreme Being, and demolish the completeness, symmetry, and harmony of his nature, and render worship impossible. The grandest of all music, the lofty chorals and anthems of the Christian Church, the 'Te Deum Laudamus' and the 'Gloria Patri', suppose all of the Divine attributes, and are prompted by the full-orbed glory of God.

3. Thirdly, since all of the Divine attributes go to make up the total glory of God, they must all of them be manifested if there is to be a complete manifestation of the Divine perfection. It is at this point that the defective view of the Divine decree which is now sought to be introduced into the Westminster Confession takes its start. The reviser of this class concedes that the Divine glory is manifested when God in the exercise of his benevolence and mercy elects many sinners to everlasting life, but denies that it is also manifested when God in the exercise

of his holiness and justice leaves some sinners to their own free will, and permits them to go down voluntarily to eternal death. He declares that election is a true doctrine, and would have it retained in the Presbyterian creed; but that reprobation is a 'horrible' doctrine, and would have it stricken out. When the confession (iii.3) asserts that 'by the decree of God, for the manifestation of his glory, some men and angels are predestined unto everlasting life', he says, Amen. But when it also asserts that 'by the decree of God, for the manifestation of his glory, some men and angels are foreordained to everlasting death', he rejects the statement as dishonoring to God. That God intends from all eternity to display his mercy in pardoning a sinner, is unobjectionable; but that he also intends from all eternity to display his justice in punishing a sinner, is vehemently opposed. The Divine love for the soul of man he thinks is worthy of God; but not the Divine wrath against the sin of man. The reviser of this class makes a selection among the Divine attributes, and confines the exhibition of the Divine glory in the Divine decree to them.

Now this one-sided and lopsided view of the Divine decree, is founded upon an erroneous view of the nature of retributive justice. It virtually implies that retributive justice does not belong to the congeries of attributes which constitute the total glory of God; and that to manifest it by leaving some sinners to their own free will in sinning, and then punishing them according to the just desert of their sin, is not a manifestation of glory but a disgrace. But the manifestation of justice is as truly a manifestation of the glory of God as the manifestation of mercy, provided both attributes belong to the Divine nature, and that both are infinitely excellent. The decree to manifest it has nothing to do with the nature of the attribute in either instance. If it is proper for God to inflict retribution at all, it is proper for him to intend to do so from all eternity. And if it is proper for God to show mercy at all, it is proper for him to intend to do so from all eternity. Justice is as morally excellent as mercy; and holiness as benevolence. All of the Divine attributes are perfect. No one is inferior to the others in this respect, because infinity characterizes them all. When God punishes impenitent and hardened Satan, and all beings who have his impenitent and hardened spirit, his act is as worthy of praise and adoration as when he pardons penitent sinners through Jesus Christ. 'I heard a great voice of much people in heaven, saying, Alleluia; Salvation, and glory, and honor, and power, unto the Lord our God; for true and righteous are his judgments' *(Rev. 19: 1, 2)*.

The view of retributive justice which we are criticizing has no support either in Scripture or in reason. St. Paul asserts that 'the ministration of death written and engraven in stones was glorious'; and that 'the ministration of condemnation is glory' *(2 Cor. 3: 7, 9)*. The ministration of death is the ministration of justice; the infliction of the righteous penalty, 'The soul that sinneth it shall die'. And the inspired apostle affirms that it is intrinsically glorious and exhibits the glory of God. It is true that he adds that 'the ministration of the Spirit' and 'the ministration of [imputed] righteousness' 'exceed in glory' the ministration of condemnation; that is, that the gospel shows more of the Divine attributes, and so is a fuller manifestation of the Divine plenitude of perfection than the legal and punitive dispensation is. But in so saying, he does not retract his proposition, that 'the ministration of condemnation is glory'. There is no need of quoting the multitude of texts that teach that holiness and justice are as grand and venerable attributes in the Divine nature, as benevolence and mercy. They excite the emotions of praise and adoration in the highest heavens. The wing-veiled seraphim emphasize these attributes in particular when they worship God in their trisagion, 'Holy, holy, holy is the Lord of Hosts'. The redeemed 'sing the song of Moses and the Lamb, saying, Great and marvellous are thy works, Lord God Almighty; just and true are thy ways, thou King of saints. Who shall not fear thee, O Lord, and glorify thy name? For thou only art holy' (*Rev. 15: 3, 4*).

The argument from reason is equally conclusive that holiness and justice constitute an essential part of the Divine character, and are august attributes that contribute to the Divine honor and glory, and therefore ought to be manifested. They are the attributes that underlie all government and legislation, human and divine. The science of law, which is next in dignity to that of theology, and in some respects is as abstruse and logical, and should therefore share in the abuse so frequently showered upon systematic theology, is built out of this quarry; and in the familiar but ever lofty and noble phrase of Hooker, the seat of law is the bosom of God, and the voice of law is the harmony of the world.

It is therefore both unscriptural and irrational to confine the manifestation of God's glory to one side of God's decree, and to some selected and favorite attributes. Within the three provinces of creation, providence, and redemption all of the attributes are manifested; and more of them are manifested in redemption than in creation and providence. And this is the best reason that can be suggested for the permission of sin. Without the sin there could be no redemption from sin, and if there had been no redemption from sin that marvellous union and combination and harmonizing of mercy with justice in the vicarious sacrifice of God incarnate and crucified, could have had no manifestation whatever. All this side of the glory of God would have been kept secret and hidden in the depths of the Godhead, and been utterly unknown to angels and men.

And here let it be noticed that the question, how many are elected and how many are reprobate, has nothing to do with the question whether God may either elect or reprobate sinners. If it is intrinsically right for him either to elect or not to elect, either to save or not to save free moral agents who by their own fault have plunged themselves into sin and ruin, numbers are of no account in establishing the rightness. And if it is intrinsically wrong, numbers are of no account in establishing the wrongness. Neither is there any necessity that the number of the elect should be small, and that of the non-elect great; or the converse. The election and the non-election, and also the numbers of the elect and the non-elect, are all alike a matter of sovereignty and optional decision. At the same time it relieves the solemnity and awfulness which overhang the decree of reprobation, to remember that the Scriptures teach that the number of the elect is much greater than that of the non-elect. The kingdom of the Redeemer in this fallen world is always described as far greater and grander than that of Satan. The operation of grace on earth is uniformly represented as mightier than that of sin. 'Where sin abounded, grace did much more abound'. And the final number of the redeemed is said to be 'a multitude which no man can number', but that of the lost is not so magnified and emphasized.

4. Fourthly, the reason why God should do everything for his own glory in the manifestation of all of his attributes, and why all of his rational creatures should do everything for the same purpose, so far as is possible to them, is because he is the first cause and the last end of all things. 'Of him, and through him, and to him, are all things', says St. Paul. Every created being and thing must have a final end; a terminus. The mineral kingdom is

made for the vegetable kingdom; the vegetable kingdom is made for the animal kingdom; the animal kingdom is made for man; and all of them together are made for God. Go through all the ranges of creation, from the molecule of matter to the seraphim, and if you ask for the final purpose of its creation, the reply is the glory of the Maker. And this is reasonable. For God is the greatest and most important, if we may use the word in such a connection, of all beings. That which justifies man in putting the dumb animals to his own uses, is the fact that he is a grander creature than they are. That which makes the inanimate world subservient to the animate; that which subsidizes the elements of earth, air, and water, and makes them tributary to the nourishment and growth of the beast and the bird, is the fact that the beast and the bird are of a higher order of existence than earth, air, and water. It was because man was the noblest, the most important, of all the creatures that God placed upon this planet, that he subordinated them all to him, and said to him in the original patent by which he deeded the globe to him: 'Behold, I have given you every herb bearing seed; have dominion over the fish of the sea, and over the fowl of the air, and over every living thing that moveth upon the earth'.

Now this principle holds good of the relation between the whole creation and its Creator. He is a higher and greater being than the whole created universe. The mass of his being, so to speak, outweighs all other masses. He never has created, he never can create, anything equal to himself in infinity and glory. And therefore it is that he is the final end, the cause of causes, the absolute terminus where all the sweep and movement of creation must come to a rest. It is an objection of the sceptic, and sometimes of those who are not sceptics, that this perpetual assertion in the Scriptures that God is the chief end of creation, and this perpetual demand that the creature glorify him, is only a species of infinite egotism; that in making the whole unlimited universe subservient to him and his purposes, the Deity is only exhibiting selfishness upon an immense scale. But this objection overlooks the fact that God is an infinitely greater and higher being than any or all of his creatures; and that from the very nature of the case the less must be subordinated to the greater. Is it egotism, when man employs in his service his ox or his ass? Is it selfishness, when the rose or the lily takes up into its own fabric and tissue the inanimate qualities of matter, and converts the dull and colorless elements of the clod into hues and odors, into beauty and bloom? There would be egotism in the procedure, if man were of no higher grade of existence than the ox or the ass. There would be selfishness, if the rose and the lily were upon the same level with the inanimate elements of matter. But the greater dignity in each instance justifies the use and the subordination. And so it is, only in an infinitely greater degree, in the case when the whole creation is subordinated and made to serve and glorify the Creator. The distance between man and his ox, between the lily and the particle of moisture which it imbibes, is measurable. It is not infinite. But the distance between God and the highest of his archangels is beyond computation. He chargeth his angels with folly. And therefore upon the principle that the less must serve the greater, the lower must be subordinate to the higher, it is right and rational that 'every.creature which is in heaven, and on the earth, and under the earth, and such as are in the sea, and all that are in them, should say: "Blessing and honor, and glory, and power be unto him that sitteth upon the throne, and unto the Lamb, for ever and ever"'.

8: The Double Predestination to Holiness and Sin

The question whether there is a double predestination to both holiness and life and sin and death, or only a single predestination to holiness and life, was raised in the fifth and sixth centuries, during the Semi-Pelagian controversy, and afterward in the ninth century, in the controversy between Gottschalk and Ratramnus on the one side, and Rabanus Maurus and Hincmar on the other. The stricter Augustinians affirmed the predestinatio duplex to both holiness and sin; the milder affirmed only the single predestination to holiness. Both alike, however, opposed the synergistic Semi-Pelagianism. The Calvinistic reformers and the Calvinistic creeds asserted the twofold predestination. The Westminster Confession declares it plainly. It is explicitly taught in Scripture. In Rom. 8: 29, it is said that 'whom God did foreknow, he also did predestinate (προώρισε) to be conformed to the image of his Son'. This is predestination to holiness. In Acts 4: 27, 28, it is said that 'against thy holy child Jesus, Herod, and Pontius Pilate, with the Gentiles and all the people of Israel were gathered, for to do whatsoever thy hand and thy counsel determined before (προώρισε) to be done'. This is predestination to sin. Compare also Acts 2: 23; Luke 22: 22; Jude 4. Precisely the same Greek word is employed in both texts, and should therefore be translated by precisely the same English word in both. James's translators render it by 'predestinate' in Rom. 8: 29, and by 'determined before' (predetermined) in Acts 4: 28. There is no material difference between 'predestinate' and 'predetermine,' but it would have been better to have employed either one word or the other in both instances, because a merely English reader might be led to suppose that two different Greek words are employed in the original. The Revisers consistently render προώρισε in both texts by the synonymous term 'foreordain'. Hetherington (Westminster Assembly, Chap. x.) contends that 'predestinate' and 'foreordain' are not synonymous and interchangeable, because in Con. iii. 3, the first is used with everlasting life, and the last with everlasting death. His statement is as follows: 'By predestination, the Westminster divines meant a particular decree determining to confer everlasting life. By foreordination, they meant a decree of order or arrangement determining that the guilty should be condemned to everlasting death; and this they regarded as the basis of judicial procedure according to which "God ordains men to dishonor and wrath for their sin". Let it furthermore be remarked that while according to this view the term predestination could never be applied to the lost, the term foreordination might be applied to the saved, since they also are subjects in one sense of judicial procedure'. There are the following objections to this denial that predestination and foreordination are equivalent terms, and to this definition of foreordination: 1. One and the same word, προώρισε, is employed in Scripture to denote the divine action in reference to both holiness and sin, life and death, and therefore if two different words are employed to translate it, they *ought* to be synonymous and applicable to both cases alike. 2. Lexicographers regard them as synonymous. Stormonth, *e.g.*, defines 'foreordain' by 'predestinate', and 'predestinate' by 'foreordain'. 3. If προώρισε, in the instance of sin and death, means only a judicial decision to punish sin, then, in the instance of holiness and life, it would mean only a judicial decision to reward holiness. If it is predestination to penalty in one case, it must be predestination to reward in the other. But when St. Paul declares that 'whom God did foreknow he did predestinate to be conformed to the image of his Son', he means that he predestinated them to the conformity itself, and not merely to the reward of it. 4. To say, as Hetherington does, that 'to foreordain some men to everlasting death' is 'a decree determining that the guilty shall be condemned to everlasting death' (*i.e.*, to the penalty of sin), is to misconceive the nature of a decree. The matter of a decree is always *optional*. It supposes the possibility of the contrary. When God decrees the creation of the world, he is at liberty not to decree it and not to create it. But when he condemns the guilty to punishment, this is not an optional matter, but follows necessarily from the nature of the divine justice and the threatening of the divine law. There is, therefore, no more place for a decree 'to condemn the guilty to everlasting death' than for a decree that virtue shall be rewardable, or that two and two shall make four. The same remark applies to Hetherington's definition of 'predestination' as 'a particular decree determining to confer everlasting life'. Everlasting life, strictly speaking, is the reward of obedience, which follows necessarily from God's promise, 'This do and thou shalt live', and from the nature of remunerative justice. There is nothing optional in it. We cannot conceive of God's decreeing not to reward obedience, and still less to punish it. Unless, therefore, 'conferring everlasting life' includes the *origination in the elect of the holiness* which is rewardable with everlasting life, as was probably the view of Hetherington, it is not the predestination which St. Paul describes as a predestination 'to be conformed to the image' of the Son of God.

In the Pauline conception, predestination, or fore-ordination, covers and includes both the holiness that is to be rewarded with life, and the sin that is to be punished with death. The holiness of the elect is predestinated, and the sin of the non-elect likewise. Both alike are represented by the apostle as standing in a certain relation to the divine purpose and the divine action, and this purpose and action are designated by the one word προώρισε. To omit both the holiness and the sin from the predestination, and retain only the recompense of each, is to mutilate the Biblical representation, and convert the divine predestination of Con. iii. 3, into the divine adjudication or sentencing of Con. iii. 7. And to omit the sin but retain the holiness, as is done by those who adopt the single predestination and reject the double, though much less defective, is yet defective in omitting that element of revealed truth contained in texts like Acts 4: 27, 28; 2: 23; Luke 22: 22; Jude 4; Rom. 9: 21, *et alia*, whereby sin as well as holiness is taken out of the sphere of chance and brought within the divine plan.

If, then, the Holy Spirit inspired St. Paul to employ the word προώρισε to denote the nature of God's action both when he predestinates the elect to holiness and the non-elect to a sin like that of crucifying the Lord of glory, it becomes a most important question: What is the nature of this predestinating action of God? What does it include and what does it exclude? The answer is, that God's predestinating in election and preterition is his making the origin of holiness in an elect sinner, and the continuance (not origin) of sin in a non-elect sinner, a *certainty* in his plan of the universe, in distinction from a *contingency* outside of that plan springing from chance; and that it includes certainty only, and excludes necessity and compulsion. Opponents of the doctrine of decrees, from the beginning, generally assume that to decree holiness or sin is to *necessitate* them. The defenders of the doctrine uniformly deny this. They contend that when the divine decree relates to the action of the human will, be it holy or sinful action, there is certainty, but not compulsion. The Westminster Confession, iii. 1, declares that 'God [fore] ordains whatsoever comes to pass; yet *so* as thereby neither is God the author of sin; nor is violence offered to the will of the creature; nor is the liberty of second causes taken away, but rather established'.

How can these things be? How, in the first place, does God make the origin and everlasting continuance of holiness in an elect sinner a certainty without compelling and necessitating his will? By the regenerating and sanctifying agency of the Holy Spirit; by 'working in the will, to will and to do of his good pleasure'. Phil. 2: 13. Scripture teaches that this operation of the Spirit does not destroy the freedom of the will. 'If the Son shall make you free, ye shall be free indeed' John 8: 36. And the report of consciousness agrees with this; for the regenerate man has no sense of being forced and unwilling in any of his experiences and exercises.

How, in the second place, does God make the everlasting continuance of sin in a non-elect sinner a certainty without compelling and necessitating his will? By letting him alone, or, in the Confessional phrase, by 'passing him by', and leaving him wholly to his own self-determination in sin? The sublapsarian preterition, which is that of the Westminster Confession and all the Reformed creeds, supposes the fall in Adam and the existence of sin to be prior, in the order of nature, to both election and preterition. Election and preterition, consequently have reference to the *continuance* of sin, not to the *origin* of it. All men fall in Adam, without exception; so that there is no election or non-election to the fall itself, but only to deliverance from it. Both election and preterition suppose the fall, and are inexplicable without it as a presupposition. Men are elected from out of a state of sin; and men are passed by and left in a state of sin. 'They who are elected [and they who are passed by] being fallen in Adam,' etc., Con. iii. 6. Election stops the continuation of sin; preterition permits the continuance of it. The non-elect man, then, like the elect, being already in the state of sin and guilt by the free fall in Adam, nothing is requisite in order to make it certain that he will for ever remain in this state but the purpose of God not to restrain and change the action of his free will and self-will in sin by regenerating it. To denominate such merely permissive action as this, compulsion, is absurd. And yet this permissive action of God secures the certainty of everlasting sin and death in the case of the non-elect, just as infallibly as the efficient action of God secures the certainty of everlasting holiness and life in the case of the elect. But in the former instance the certainty is secured wholly by the action of the sinner himself, while in the latter instance it is secured by the action of the Holy Spirit within the sinner. This leaving of the sinful will to its own movement makes endless sin an infallible certainty. For the sinner himself will and can never regenerate himself; and if God has in his sovereignty decided and purposed not to regenerate him, his willing and endless continuance in sin and death is certain. Every Christian knows that if, in his unregeneracy, he had been left wholly to his own free will, without any restraint from God, he would infallibly have gone from bad to worse for ever and ever.

In these two ways of efficiency and permission, God 'foreordains' and makes certain two things that unquestionably 'come to pass,' namely, the everlasting holiness and life of some men, and the everlasting sin and death of some men; 'yet *so* as thereby God is not the author of sin; nor is violence done to the will of the creature; nor is the liberty of second causes taken away, but rather established'. When God predetermined from eternity not to restrain and prevent 'Herod, and Pontius Pilate, with the Gentiles, and all the people of Israel', from crucifying his beloved Son, but to leave them to their own wicked inclination and voluntary action in the case, he made this crucifixion a certainty, but not a necessity, as is evinced by the 'woe' pronounced upon them by the Son of God. Luke 22: 22. Men with hearts and dispositions full of hatred toward the Saviour of the world, if left to themselves are infallibly certain to cry, 'Crucify him; crucify him'. John 19: 6–15.

The Confession (vi. 1; L.C. 19) declared that God 'permits' sin, but that it is not a 'bare permission'. Con. v. 4. The permission that is adopted by the Assembly is one that occurs by a voluntary decision of God which he need not have made, had he so pleased. He might have decided not to permit sin; in which case it would not have entered his universe. The 'bare permission' which is rejected by the Assembly means that God makes no voluntary decision at all in the case; that he could not have prevented the fall of angels and men, but stands 'like an idle spectator', having no control over the event which he witnesses. Augustine makes the following statement in his Enchiridion, Ch. 100: 'In a way unspeakably strange and wonderful, even what is done in opposition to God's will [of desire] does not defeat his will [of decree]. For it would not be done did he not permit it, and of course his permission is not unwilling, but willing; nor would a Good Being permit evil to be done except that in his omnipotence he can turn evil into good'. Calvin, adopting Augustine's phraseology, concisely marks the difference between the two permissions in the remark, that 'God's permission of sin is not involuntary, but voluntary' Inst. I. xviii. 3. Both Augustine and Calvin had particular reference, in this connection, to the first origin of sin in angels and men.[1] But their statement holds true of the continuance of sin in angels and men. When God passes by all the fallen and sinful angels, and does not regenerate and save any of them, it is by a positive voluntary decision that might have been different had he so pleased. He could have saved them. And when God passes by some fallen and sinful men and does not regenerate and save them, this also is a positive voluntary decision that might have been different had he so pleased. He could have saved them. To deny this option of God in either instance is to deny, first, the divine sovereignty in the exercise of mercy; and, second, the divine omnipotence in the control of creatures.

---

[1] The permissive decree as related to the *origin* of sin presents a difficulty that does not exist in reference to the *continuance* of sin. The certainty of the continuance of sin in fallen man is easily explained, by merely leaving the fallen will to its self-determination. But merely leaving the unfallen will to its self-determination would not make its apostasy certain; because it was endowed by creation with a power to remain holy as created, and there was no punitive withdrawal of any grace given in creation until after apostasy. How, under these circumstances a permissive decree which does not operate by direct efficiency can make the fall of a holy being certain, is an inscrutable mystery. Respecting it, Turretin (VI. vii. 1) makes the following remark: 'Two extremes are to be avoided. First, that of defect, when an otiose permission of sin is ascribed to God. Second, that of excess, when the causality of sin is ascribed to him. Between these extremes, the orthodox hold the mean, who contend that the providence of God extends to sin in such way that he does not involuntarily permit it, as the Pelagians say, nor actively cause it as the Libertines assert, but voluntarily ordains and controls it'.

9: *Common and Special Grace*

The distinction between common and special grace is closely connected with the Calvinistic doctrine of election and preterition. If it is denied or explained away, it is impossible to hold the Calvinistic view on these latter points. This will appear by considering the distinction as taught in Scripture, and formulated in the Westminster Standards.

Common grace is a lower degree of grace than special. The latter succeeds in overcoming the enmity of the carnal mind and the opposition of the sinful will; the former does not succeed. Says John Howe, 'When divine grace is working but at the common rate; then it suffers itself oftentimes to be overcome, and yields the victory to the contending sinner'. This was the case with the people of Israel as described by Stephen, 'Ye stiff-necked and uncircumcised in heart and ears, ye do always resist the Holy Ghost: as your fathers did, so do ye'. Acts 7: 51. The same complaint was made against resisting Israel by Isaiah, 'They rebelled and vexed his Holy Spirit; therefore he was turned to be their enemy' Isa. 63: 10. The same failure of common grace to subdue the sinner is noted in Gen. 6: 3, 'My Spirit shall not always strive with man'. Whenever man quenches conviction of sin and plunges into temptation in order to get rid of serious and anxious thoughts, and the Holy Spirit leaves him to his own self-will, this is common grace. The process is described in the solemn words of God himself, 'Because I have called and ye have refused; I have stretched out my hand and no man regarded, but ye have set at nought all my counsel and would none of my reproof, I also will laugh at your calamity, I will mock when your fear cometh' Prov. 1: 24–26. In common grace, the sinner is too obstinate and self-determined in sin for it to succeed.

In special grace, on the other hand, the Holy Spirit does not leave the sinner to his own self-determination, but continues to operate upon his resisting will until he subdues it. He 'makes him willing in the day of his power' Ps. 110: 3. He 'works in him to will and to do of his good pleasure' Phil. 2: 13. He 'makes him perfect in every good work to do his will, working in him that which is well pleasing in his sight' Heb. 13: 21. This grade of divine grace is higher than common grace. It is denominated 'irresistible', not in the sense that no resistance is made by the sinner, but in the sense that it conquers all his resistance. It is also denominated 'effectual', because it secures salvation. It is also called 'regenerating', because it changes the disposition of the sinful heart and will by 'the washing of regeneration and renewing of the Holy Ghost'. Tit. 3: 5.

These two forms and grades of grace, so plainly described in the Scripture texts above cited, are mentioned in the Westminster Confession, vii. 3, 'Man by his fall, having made himself incapable of life by that [legal] covenant, the Lord was pleased to make a second, commonly called the covenant of grace, wherein he freely offereth unto sinners life and salvation by Jesus Christ, requiring of them faith in him, that they may be saved, and promising to give unto all those that are ordained to life his Holy Spirit, to make them willing and able to believe'. According to this statement there are two things contained in the covenant of grace: (*a*) An *offer to sinners of life and salvation by Jesus Christ, requiring of them* faith in

[93]

him, that they may be saved; and (*b*) a *promise* to give unto all those that are ordained to life the Holy Spirit, to make them willing and able to believe. The 'offer' in the covenant of grace is made to all sinners without exception, but the 'promise' in the covenant is made only to 'those that are ordained to life', or the elect. The 'offer' is common grace; the 'promise' is special grace. The 'offer' is taught in such Scriptures as, 'Go ye into all the world and preach the gospel to every creature. He that believeth shall be saved'. Mark 16: 15. 'God so loved the world that he gave his only begotten Son, that whosoever believeth in him should not perish, but have everlasting life'. John 3: 16. The 'promise' is taught in such Scriptures as, 'A new heart also will I give you, and a new spirit will I put within you, and I will take away the stony heart out of your flesh, and I will give you an heart of flesh'. Ezek. 36: 26, 27. 'All that the Father giveth me shall come to me; and him that cometh to me [because given by the Father] I will in no wise cast out. No man can come to me, except the Father which hath sent me, draw him'. John 6: 37, 44.

The following then, are some of the marks of distinction between common and special grace: (*a*) In common grace God demands faith in Christ, but does not give it; in special grace God both demands and gives faith, for 'faith is the gift of God'. Eph. 2: 8. When God says to a sinner: 'Believe on the Lord Jesus Christ, and thou shalt be saved', he makes no promise or pledge to originate faith in him. The sinner, in this case, must originate his own faith, and any sinner that originates it will find that God will be true to his word. (*b*) In common grace man must of himself fulfil the condition of salvation, namely, believe and repent; in special grace God persuades and enables him to fulfil it. (*c*) In common grace the call to believe and repent is invariably ineffectual, because man is averse to faith and repentance and in bondage to sin; in special grace the call is invariably effectual, because his aversion and bondage are changed into willingness and true freedom by the operation of the Holy Spirit. (*d*) Common grace is universal and indiscriminate, having no relation to election and preterition. No man is elected to it, and no man is 'passed by' in its bestowment. All men who come to years of self-consciousness are more or less convicted of sin (*Rom. 1: 32; 2: 14, 15*), are more or less commanded to repent (*Acts 17: 30*), are more or less urged to repentance (*Rom. 2: 4*), and are more or less striven with by the Holy Spirit (*Gen. 6: 3; Acts 17: 26, 27*) – all of which belong to the common operations of divine grace. Special grace, on the contrary, is particular and discriminating, and is connected with election and preterition. God does not originate faith and repentance in all men, nor does he promise to do so. He does not persuade and enable every man without exception to believe and repent. Only those whom he chooses before the foundation of the world are the subjects of that higher degree of the energy of the Holy Ghost by which these wonderful effects are wrought in the sinner. Respecting special grace, God 'saith to Moses, I will have mercy on whom I will have mercy, and I will have compassion on whom I will have compassion'. And St. Paul from this draws the inference, 'Therefore he hath mercy on whom he will have mercy, and whom he will he hardeneth' [leaves in sin]. Rom. 9: 15, 18. In accordance with these and similar scriptures, the Confession (vii. 3) declares that it is only to 'those that are ordained to life' that God 'promises to give his Holy Spirit to make them willing and able to believe'.

What now is the difference between the Calvinistic and the Arminian view of common grace? This is a question of great importance just now, because the Northern Presbyterian Church has decided by a large majority that it will make no alteration of its Standards that will impair their

Calvinism. Calvinism asserts that common grace cannot be made successful by the *co-operation* of the unregenerate sinner with the Holy Spirit, and thereby be converted into special or saving grace: Arminianism asserts that it can be. The Arminian contends that the ordinary operations of the Divine Spirit which are experienced by all men indiscriminately will succeed, if the unrenewed man will cease to resist them and will yield to them. Ceasing to resist and yielding, he contends, is an agency which the natural man can and must exert of himself, and this agency co-working with that of the Holy Spirit secures the result – namely, faith and repentance. Faith and repentance are thus the product of a joint agency: that of God and that of the unregenerate sinner. Neither party originates faith and repentance alone. Neither party is independent of the other in this transaction. If the sinner does not cease resisting and submit, God will fail, and if God does not assist him by common grace, the sinner will fail. Each conditions the other; and consequently the Arminian, from his point of view, is consistent in asserting that the Divine election to faith and repentance is not sovereign and independent of the sinner's action but is conditioned by it.

The Calvinist, on the contrary, holds that the unregenerate man never ceases to resist and never yields to God of his own motion, but only as he is acted upon by the Holy Spirit and is thereby 'persuaded and enabled' to cease resisting and to yield obedience. Ceasing to resist God, he contends, is *holy* action, and so is yielding or submitting to God. To refer this kind of action to the sinful and unregenerate will as its author, the Calvinist asserts is contrary to the Scripture declaration, that 'the carnal mind is enmity against God, and is not subject to the law of God, neither indeed can be'. Rom. 8: 7. A will at enmity with God never of itself ceases resisting him, and never of itself yields to him. It must be changed from enmity into love by 'the washing of regeneration and renewing of the Holy Ghost' in order to sweet and gentle submission. The sinner, as such, cannot, therefore, assist and co-operate with the Holy Spirit in this work of originating faith and repentance, but the whole of it must be done by that Almighty Agent who can turn the human heart as the rivers of water. Christ, through the Spirit, is the sole 'author of faith' (*Heb. 12: 2*). When the Holy Spirit puts forth a higher degree of his energy than he exerts in his ordinary operation, he overcomes and stops the sinner's resistance instead of the sinner's overcoming and stopping it of himself, and inclines the sinner to yield to the Divine monitions and impulse instead of the sinner's yielding of his own accord. If the sinner's resistance is 'overcome', it is overcome by God's action; but if it 'ceases', it ceases by the sinner's action. To say that common grace would succeed if it were not resisted by man, is not the same as saying that common grace would succeed if it were yielded to by man. Non-resistance is different from ceasing resistance. In the former instance there is no opposition by the man; in the latter there is opposition, which is put a stop to by the man.

The doctrine of a co-operating and conditioning action of the unrenewed sinner, by which common grace may become special or saving grace, so that all mankind stand in the same relation to election, and there is no preterition by God, because the difference between the elect and the non-elect is not made by the Divine decree, but by man's action in yielding or not yielding to common grace, is clearly expressed in the following extract from the Confession of the Arminian Remonstrants: 'Although there is the greatest diversity in the degrees in which grace is bestowed in accordance with the Divine will, yet the Holy Spirit confers, or at least is ready to confer, upon all and each to whom the Word is ordinarily preached, as much grace as is sufficient for generating faith and carrying forward their conversion in its successive stages. This sufficient grace for faith and conversion is allotted not only to those who actually believe and are converted, but *also to those who do not actually believe*, and are not in fact converted. So that there is no decree of absolute reprobation' (Confession, ch. xvii.). This view of grace is synergistic. Every man that hears the gospel receives a degree of grace that is sufficient for generating faith and repentance, provided he yields to it. If, therefore, he does not believe and repent, it must be because of the absence of some *human* efficiency to co-operate with the Divine; and therefore the difference between the saved and the lost, the elect and the non-elect, is partly referable to the human will, and not wholly to the Divine decree. So far as the Divine influence is concerned, the saved and the lost stand upon the same common position and receive the same common form and degree of grace, which is sufficient to save provided it be rightly used and assisted by the sinner. The saved man makes the common grace effectual by an act of his own will, namely, yielding and ceasing resistance; while the lost man nullifies it by an act of his own will, namely, persisting in enmity and opposition. According to the monergistic or Calvinistic view of grace, on the contrary, no man receives a grace that is 'sufficient for generating faith' who does not receive such a measure of Divine influence as *overcomes* his hostile will; so that he does not stop his own resistance but is stopped by the mercy and power of God; so that his faith and repentance are not the result in part of his own efficiency, but solely of the Holy Spirit's irresistible and sovereign energy in regeneration. In a word, the dependence upon Divine grace in the Calvinistic system is total; in the Arminian is partial. In the former, common grace cannot be made saving grace by the sinner's co-action; in the latter it can be.

It is an open question between the two great evangelical divisions of the Christian Church which of these two views of grace is more correct and more conformed to Scripture. But it is not an open question whether one view is the same thing as the other. Yet the discussion respecting the revision of the Westminster Standards shows that some who claim to be Calvinists adopt the doctrine of co-operation, and make election and salvation depend partly upon human action. Consider the following statement of an advocate of revision: 'There is a human and a divine side to regeneration. God determines how many and who will be saved, and every man determines for himself whether he will be among that number'. Here are two 'determiners' who co-operate in regeneration, God and the sinner. And if the sinner 'determines for himself whether he will be among the number of the saved', then certainly it is not God who 'determines how many and who will be saved'. It is the sinner who determines this. This is not Calvinism.

Common grace is connected with God's legislative will, or will of desire; special grace with his decretive will, or will of purpose. (See p. 50, note.) These two modes of the Divine will are presented by St. Paul and St. Peter in two passages that are often misapprehended. The texts, 'God our Saviour will have all men to be saved, and to come to the knowledge of the truth' (*1 Tim. 2: 3, 4*), and 'the Lord is long-suffering to us-ward, not willing that any should perish, but that all should come to repentance' (*2 Pet. 3: 9*), are often quoted as if they were identical in their teaching, and as if both refer to common grace. An examination will show that the first text is universal in its meaning, and refers to the general offer of the gospel; but the last is particular, and relates to the effectual call and actual salvation of the elect alone.

In I Tim. 2: 4, the Greek is ὃς πάντας ἀνξρώπους ξέλει σωξῆναι (who desires all men to be saved). In 2 Pet. 3: 9, it is μὴ βουλόμενός τινας ἀπολέσξαι, ἀλλὰ πάντας εἰς μετύνοιαν χωρῆσαι (not purposing that some should perish, but that all should go on to [perfect] repentance). The employment of ξέλω in the first passage, and of βούλομαι in the second, indicates the first point of difference. The former denotes the will of desire, the latter the will of purpose. An examination of the texts in Bruder's Concordance will plainly show that in the New Testament this is generally the use of these two words. The Septuagint use is not so strict as that of the New Testament, and the classical is still more loose. The distinction generally given by lexicographers is, that βούλομαι involves deliberation and intention along with desire ('deliberato consilio aliquid volo, cupio, decerno'), while ξέλω denotes simple desire only ('simpliciter volo'). In I Tim. 2: 4, St. Paul declares that God 'desires all men to be saved', but not that he purposes that they all shall be. In 2 Pet. 3: 9, St. Peter declares that God 'does not purpose that some [of us] should perish, but that all [of us] should go on to repentance' (complete sanctification).

And this brings us to the second point of difference. The action of ξέλει in I Tim. 2: 4 terminates on πάντας ἀνξρώπους; that of βουλόμενος in 2 Pet. 3: 9 terminates on τινας (ἀνξρώπους). All men are the object of the Divine desire; some are the object of the Divine decree. Who these latter are is shown by the immediately preceding context, 'The Lord is long-suffering to us-ward (εἰς ἡμᾶς), not purposing that any [of us: ἡμῶν] should perish'. St. Paul is writing to the children of God, and it is concerning such that he affirms that none of them shall perish, because this is the decretive will of God.

It is to be regretted that the terms desire or inclination, and purpose, intention, or decree, have not been more carefully employed in both the Authorized and Revised versions to mark the difference between ξέλημα and βούλημα. In Rom. 9: 22, the meaning of St. Paul would be more clearly expressed if the translation were, 'What if God, [though] inclined (ξέλων) to shew his wrath and make his power known, [yet] endured with much long-suffering the vessels of wrath fitted for destruction'. The apostle asks the objector what he would say in reply if the fact were (as it actually is), that God shows infinite patience and forbearance toward the obstinate and im-penitent sinner in putting a restraint upon his holy displeasure against sin, which inclines him to the immedi-ate punishment of it. In Rom. 9: 19, the meaning would be free from all ambiguity if the rendering were, 'Who hath resisted his decree (βουλήματι)?'. Every human being has resisted God's 'will' in the sense of desire, as used in Matt. 5: 10, 'Thy will (ξέλημα) be done'. In Heb. 6: 17, the writer's thought would be more exactly presented if the rendering were, 'Wherein God, intending (βουλόμενος) more abundantly to show unto the heirs of promise the immutability of his counsel,' etc. The rendering in the Authorized version, 'willing to show,' might mean willing in distinction from unwilling, or willing in the sense of desiring, neither of which expresses the definite purpose of God in the case. The Revised version renders, 'being minded to show'. But 'minded' denotes desire and inclination rather than purpose or intention; as in Rom. 8: 6, 'To be carnally minded is death, but to be spiritually minded is life and peace'. In Matt. 1: 19, both ξέλω and βούλομαι are found, and would be precisely translated in this manner: 'Then Joseph her husband being a just [law-respecting] man, and [yet] not wishing (ξέλων) to make her a public example, intended (ἐβουλήξη) to put her away privily'.

10: *The True Proportion in a Creed between the Universal and the Special Love of God*

It is objected that insufficient emphasis is laid in the Westminster Confession upon the universal offer of mercy, and the common call to faith and repentance, and some even contend that these are not contained in it. Advocates of revision demand that these doctrines shall be more particularly enunciated than they now are, and complain that more is said concerning the electing love of God in the effectual call than upon his indiscriminate love in the outward call. In reply to this, we mention the three following reasons why the Westminster Confession, in common with all the Reformed creeds, is more full and emphatic regarding the special love of God toward his church than regarding his general love toward the world.

1. The Scriptures themselves are more full and emphatic in the first reference than in the last. A careful examination of the Old and New Testaments will show that while the universal compassion of God toward sinful men is plainly and frequently taught, yet it is the relation of God as the Saviour of his people that constitutes the larger proportion of the teachings of the Prophets, the Psalms, the Gospels, and the Epistles. These parts of Scripture are full of God's dealings with his covenant people, instructing them, expostulating with them, rebuking them, comforting them, helping them – expressing in these and other ways his special love and affection

for them, as those whom he has chosen before the foundation of the world. Throughout the Bible men universally are both invited and commanded to believe and repent. No one disputes this. This is God's universal love. But, whenever the love of God is particularly enlarged upon, carefully delineated, and repeatedly emphasized, in the great majority of instances it is his electing love. The Saviour's last discourses with his disciples, and his last prayer, have for their principal theme the 'love of his own which were in the world', whom 'he loved unto the end'. For these he specially supplicates. 'I pray for them: I pray not [now] for the world, but for them which thou hast given me, for they are thine.' The Epistles of Paul also are like the Redeemer's discourses. So full are they of expanded and glowing descriptions of the electing love of God that the charge of a narrow Jewish conception of the Divine compassion is frequently made against them. The Confession therefore follows the Scriptures in regard to the *proportion* of doctrine, when it puts the mercy of God toward his people in the foreground. And to object to this proportion is to object to Divine Revelation.

2. The electing love of God and his special grace naturally has the foremost place in the Confession as in Scripture, because it is the only love and grace that is *successful* with the sinner. The universal love of God in his outward call and common grace is a failure, because it is inadequate to overcome the enmity and resistance with which man meets it. While therefore the sacred writers represent the common call as prompted by the compassion of God toward the sinner, and expressive of his sincere desire that he would hear it, and as aggravating his persistence in the sin of which a free pardon is offered, yet inasmuch as it yields no saving and blessed results, they see no reason for making it the principal and prominent part of the Divine oracles. But that electing love in the

effectual call and irresistible grace, which overcomes the aversion of the sinner and powerfully inclines his hostile will, inasmuch as it is the principal work of God in the human heart, becomes the principal subject of discourse for 'the holy men of God who spake as they were moved by the Holy Ghost'. They dwell rather on the special grace that triumphs over human depravity, than on the common grace that is defeated by it.

3. The universal offer of mercy is not emphasized and enlarged upon in the Confession, because this is *superfluous*. That the offer of mercy in Christ is universal goes without saying, because if offered at all it *must* be offered universally. It is impossible to offer the atonement of Christ only to the elect. No man knows who are the elect, and therefore the ambassador of Christ must offer salvation to everybody or else to nobody. Any offer at all must, from the nature of the case, be unlimited. Why, therefore, waste words in a creed to declare with unnecessary fulness what must be as a matter of course, and what is clearly and sufficiently announced in such Scripture entreaties as 'Turn ye, turn ye, for why will ye die', and such Confessional declarations as we have cited on pp. 23–28?

If it be objected that God knows who are the elect, and that it is inconsistent in *him* to make a universal offer of mercy through an ignorant agent like a Christian minister, when he does not purpose to regenerate and save every individual man, this is a difficulty for him, not for man. It is certainly consistent for man to offer mercy indiscriminately because he does not know who are the elect, even if it is not for God because he does know. But *is* it inconsistent for God? What are the facts in relation to God? He offers mercy to a man in the outward call, and accompanies this call with that degree of grace denominated 'common'. The man despises the call and frustrates the grace, by suppressing conviction of sin and persisting in the worldly life which he loves. Now does the fact that God has decided not to do anything more than this toward the salvation of this resisting man prove that in doing *this* he has acted inconsistently with mercy? Is not God's action up to this point kind, forbearing, patient, and merciful? All that he has done to this man in the outward call and common grace has had no tendency to injure him by confirming him in sin, but, on the contrary, to benefit him by delivering him from it. There has been nothing hard or unmerciful in this form and grade of divine grace toward this guilty sinner who does not deserve the least degree of grace. It is true that it is not the highest form of grace, yet it is real grace, and far greater than any sinner merits. Is it inconsistent in God to do any kind and degree of good to a sinner, if he has decided not to do the highest kind and degree of good in his power? Shall God do nothing at all that is kind and gracious to a sinful man, unless he has decided to overcome all the opposition that he may make to his kindness and grace? Must God make no offer of mercy to a sinner, unless he has decided to make him accept it? Shall he extend the common call only in the case in which he intends to follow it with the effectual call?

There never was an age of the world when men more needed than now to be reminded that they are resisting the common grace of God, and rejecting his universal offer of mercy, and that in so doing they run the great hazard of God's *preterition*; of being passed by in the bestowment of regenerating grace. Men need to fear, lest, by stifling conviction of sin and turning a deaf ear to the common call, they shall never be the subjects of the effectual call in regeneration. For, says the Larger Catechism, 68, 'others [than the elect] may be, and often are outwardly called by the ministry of the word, and have some common operations of the Spirit, who, for their wilful neglect and contempt of the grace offered to them, being justly *left* in their unbelief, do never truly come to Jesus Christ'. And this agrees with the solemn declaration of God himself: 'Because I have called and ye refused; I have stretched out my hand, and no man regarded; I also will laugh at your calamity' (*Prov. 1: 24–26*).

11: *Infant Salvation as Related to Original Sin*

In order to a correct understanding of the Calvinistic doctrine of the salvation of infants, it is necessary to remember the two theories of original sin which began in the Augustinian and Semi-Pelagian anthropologies, and are continued in the Calvinistic and Arminian. They differ essentially from each other, and result in essentially different views of infant salvation.

The Augustinian doctrine is that original sin is damning, and that infants deserve eternal death on account of it. Being fallen in Adam, they have a corrupt disposition or inclination, which is both voluntary and responsible. It is the self in its central and inmost self-determination. Though the infant has committed no acts of known and wilful transgression, yet his heart is estranged from God, and his will is at enmity with the holy law of God. When he comes to years of consciousness he *feels* guilty for this estrangement and this enmity, and this proves that it *is* guilt. An infant, therefore, needs salvation because he is really culpable and punishable. He requires the whole work of the Redeemer, both as expiating guilt and cleansing from pollution.

The Semi-Pelagian doctrine is, that original sin is not damning; that neither infants nor adults deserve eternal punishment on account of it. Only actual transgression merits hell. Upon this theory original sin is calamitous, not culpable, and therefore the dying infant is not in a strictly damnable and lost condition. He has a disordered nature which tempts and prompts to sin, but is not sin itself. Consequently when he is said to be 'saved', the term does not mean, as it does on the other theory, that he is delivered from the pains of hell as something that might justly be inflicted upon him.

If the first of these views of original sin is adopted, the salvation of dying infants, whether of some or of all, is an act of unobliged and unmerited grace. It is salvation from deserved eternal death. By reason of original sin the infant is truly culpable before the law and justice of God. He might be punished eternally for it, and no injustice would be done to him. His salvation, therefore, is as unmerited and optional as that of an adult. God has a just liberty to decide whether he will leave all infants in sin and misery, or whether he will regenerate and save all of them or a part of them. These things follow if the premise that original sin is guilt is correct.

If the second of these views of original sin is adopted, the 'salvation' of dying infants is not real but nominal and putative, because it is not grace but debt. If there be no culpability in original sin, there is none resting upon the infant; for this is all the sin he has. If he does not deserve hell punishment, he does not need to be saved from it, and is not saved from it. His moral condition is one of misfortune, not of guilt. His so-called 'salvation', therefore, cannot be regulated like that of an adult by the sovereign, unobliged, and optional decision of God. No infants can justly be sent to perdition for original sin. All must be 'saved' from its consequences, whatever these may be. These are the necessary inferences from this view of original sin, and they are embodied in the declaration that 'it would be unjust and wrong in God to send innocent and harmless infants to perdition'.

Now, it is plain that whichever of these two views of

original sin be correct, the doctrine of infant salvation cannot be the same upon one that it is upon the other. Neither can there be a blending or mixing of one with the other. It is sometimes said that the extension of election by the later Calvinism, so as to include all infants as a class instead of a part of them as individuals, is a departure from the Calvinistic system, and a considerable modification of it in the direction of Arminianism. But there is nothing of this, *provided the Calvinistic view of original sin is retained strictly and fully.* So long as the later Calvinist holds with the elder, that 'every sin, both *original* and actual, being a transgression of the righteous law of God, doth in its own nature bring *guilt* upon the sinner, whereby he is bound over to the *wrath of God*, and made subject to *death*, *temporal* and *eternal*' (Confess. vi. 6), he stands upon the very same theological ground with him. He adopts the same definitions of sin, of guilt, of salvation, of grace, of regeneration, and of election. The only point of difference is the minor one relating to the diameter of the circle of election. The only question between the parties is, How many guilty and lost dying infants does the infinite and unmerited mercy of God regenerate and save from eternal death? Though the elder Calvinist did not, like the later, say that infant salvation is classical, not individual, he yet prepared the way for it, by distinguishing between infants that are saved by 'covenanted' mercy and those that are saved by 'uncovenanted'. Even Augustine indirectly worked toward this widening of the circle of infant election in his assertion that the sufferings of lost infants are 'mitissima omnium'. He held with great positiveness that original sin in an infant is the inclination of the will descending and inherited from Adam, and as such is free agency and wrong agency, and as such is punishable with the just penalty of sin. It would therefore have been more self-consistent and logical in him, not to have *minimized* as he did the punishment due to original sin in an infant, but rather to have *magnified* the divine mercy in saving all infants from it instead of only a part of them. It would have been more self-consistent and logical, we say, because the verdict of justice is a fixed quantity respecting the intrinsic demerit of original sin, whether in an infant or an adult, and may be neither increased nor diminished, but mercy may be more or less. Justice cannot give two decisions as to whether original sin *deserves* eternal death; but mercy can give two decisions as to whether it will or will not *pardon* it. Augustine might therefore have affirmed the exact and full retribution due to original sin in the case of infants as in that of adults, and then have affirmed with the later Calvinist that the infinite compassion of God frees all of them from the dreadful guilt and penalty by the blood of atonement. In this instance, where sin abounded grace would superabound. The greater the penalty to which the infant is exposed, the greater the mercy in remitting it. The salvation of an infant in this case means something. Infant salvation is real; for it is the deliverance of a soul that is really guilty and liable to endless woe. And it is costly; for it is by the sacrificial death of God incarnate.

But if the other view of original sin, namely, that it is not properly sin, and does not deserve or bring eternal death, is adopted in connection with the universal salvation of dying infants, then indeed there will be a very great departure from the Calvinistic system. Another meaning is given to 'sin' and to 'salvation'. The evil from which the infant is 'saved' is very small, and the kindness showed to him is very small also. A 'painted sinner', as Luther said, has only a 'painted Saviour'. It was this view of original sin as not damning, that made many Calvinists in the seventeenth century afraid to affirm the salvation of all infants; because at that time the two views were combined together by the Arminians. Arminian advocates of universal infant salvation rested it upon the ground that it would be unjust to condemn infants to perdition solely because of original sin. Their Calvinistic opponents, such as Owen, for example, regarded this as a fatal error, leading logically to conclusions respecting the nature of sin and salvation, from which probably some of the evangelical Arminians themselves would have shrunk. Had the doctrine of the guilt and damnability of original sin in infants been conceded, it is highly probable that Calvinists generally of that century might have been more ready, with Calvinists generally of this, to make the circle of election large enough to include all dying infants, and not a part only. For they had no disposition to contract and minimize the extent of God's decree of election, but every disposition to widen it, provided Scripture gave warrant for it. In the present controversy respecting the revision of the Westminster Standards, this difference between the two views of original sin should be kept distinctly in mind. The Confession is explicit in teaching the culpability of original sin; and we have seen no proposition to strike this teaching out of it. This tenet, consequently, must go along with that of infant salvation. The mercy of God saves the 'little children' from the very same common depravity and guilt that is in their parents, and from the very same dreadful penalty that righteously overhangs 'the carnal mind, which is enmity against God, is not subject to the law of God, neither indeed can be' (*Rom. 8: 7*). In this case, the mercy of God is immense, because it pardons and eradicates an immense sin; for the sin of heart and inclination is greater than that of act and outward conduct, because it is the source and poison of the whole of it. On the other theory, the mercy of God is small; for the only sin that is really forgiven, is that of actual transgression.

The doctrine of the damnation of infants is tempered and mitigated by that of their salvation. This is often overlooked, either ignorantly or designedly, by the opponents of Calvinism. It does not follow that because a human being *deserves* to go to hell for sin, he actually will go there. His sin may be pardoned and eradicated. The truth, but not the *whole* truth, is told, when it is merely said that Calvinism teaches the damnation of infants. It teaches their salvation also. This is true even if the salvation is only of the infants of believers, as in the elder Calvinism; and is still more so, if the salvation is of all infants as in the later Calvinism. When, therefore, the enemy of this creed stops with the first statement, he is like a false witness in court, who after relating one fact is silent upon another which ought to be mentioned along with it, and which is requisite in order to put the judge and jury in possession of the whole case. A falsehood may be told concerning a theological system, as well by not speaking the whole truth, as by uttering a direct lie. And there is considerable of such falsehood current. Augustine and Calvin both held that infants, like adults, are children of Adam, responsibly sinned and fell with him in the first transgression, and are justly involved with him in the same condemnation to eternal death. 'In Adam all die', I Cor. 15: 22. But both alike held that the saving grace of God pardons and eradicates original sin in infants, upon the same *principles*, and by the same method of *election* that it pardons and eradicates any and all sin, namely, through the vicarious satisfaction of Christ and the regenerating operation of the Holy Spirit. It is true that they did not find proof in Scripture that infant election is classical, and therefore left it individual like that of adults. But had they, like their successors in the Modern church, seen reason in the Word of God for believing that the Divine mercy is extended to all infants as infants, instead of to a part, they would have gladly affirmed this. It is only a question of exegesis between them and their successors; and this turns upon the point whether the Saviour's declaration, 'Of such is the kingdom of God', means, 'Of *all* such', or, 'Of *some* of such'.

On page 132 we contend that the first is the most natural understanding of the words of Christ, and we also think that it is the most natural understanding of the Assembly's phraseology respecting 'elect infants dying in infancy'. There are two interpretations of this Confessional phrase. One makes the antithesis to be, 'non-elect infants dying in infancy'; the other makes it to be, 'elect infants not dying in infancy'. According to the first view, the contrast is between the elect and the non-elect, in which case the election of dying infants is individual. There are some non-elect dying infants. According to the second, it is between two different classes of the elect, in which case the election of dying infants is classical. There are no non-elect dying infants. That the second view is the correct one is evident, for the following reasons:

1. Whenever the contrast between the elect and non-elect is intended in the Westminster Standards, both classes are particularly mentioned and particularly described. See Con. iii. 3, 6, 7; L.C. 13, 68. But in Con. x. 3, when dying infants are spoken of, mention is made only of the elect, and a description is given of them alone. In view, therefore, of the fact that the Assembly invariably mention and describe the non-elect in connection with the elect, whenever, in their opinion, there are any non-elect, the natural inference from this silence of the Assembly concerning non-elect dying infants is, that they did not mean to teach that there are any.

2. All of the elect are elected as infants in the womb. Jer. 1: 5; Luke 1: 15; Rom. 9: 10–12; Gal. 1: 15. There is no election of men as adults or in adult years. Consequen-

tly, the phrase 'elect infants' is the only one that designates the entire body of the elect. As in law, 'infants' means all persons under age, so in the Westminster theology, 'elect infants' means all persons who are chosen to eternal life 'before the foundation of the world'. This being so, 'elect infants' fall into three classes with reference to the time of their death and their regeneration. (*a*) 'Elect infants' who die in infancy and are regenerated in infancy. (*b*) 'Elect infants' who do not die in infancy but are regenerated in infancy. (*c*) 'Elect infants' who do not die in infancy but are regenerated in years of discretion. The object of the declaration in Con. x. 3, is to describe the manner in which the regeneration of the first class of 'elect infants' (and, incidentally, also of the second) is effected as compared with that of the third class. It declares that such 'elect infants' as die in infancy 'are regenerated and saved by Christ through the Spirit', without the outward call and conviction of sin. This distinguishes them (and also, incidentally, the second class, who also are regenerated in infancy but do not die in infancy) from the third class of 'elect infants', who come to years of discretion, and not having been regenerated in infancy, are then 'regenerated and saved by Christ through the Spirit', in connection with the outward call and conviction of sin by the law, written or unwritten. The true antithesis, consequently, to 'elect infants dying in infancy' is 'elect infants not dying in infancy', and not non-elect infants dying in infancy.

That this is the correct interpretation of the phrase, 'elect infants', is corroborated by the fact that the original draft of the tenth chapter of the Confession did not contain this third section, being wholly silent concerning dying elect infants and elect heathen; and the Assembly instructed its committee to insert a section relating (*a*) to the manner of regeneration when there can be no outward call by the ministry of the Word and no conviction of sin, as in the case of elect infants dying in infancy; and (*b*) to the manner of regeneration in the case of 'all other elect persons who are incapable of being outwardly called by the ministry of the [written] Word', but who are capable of conviction of sin through the instrumentality of the unwritten. These latter belong to the third class of 'elect infants'. An adult heathen who was elected in infancy but not regenerated in infancy, is 'regenerated by Christ through the Spirit who worketh when, and where, and how he pleaseth'. The regeneration in this instance occurs in adult years, and is effected in connection with conviction of sin; but the instrument employed by the divine Spirit in this conviction is not the written law, but the unwritten, spoken of by St. Paul in Rom. 2: 14, 15.

12: The Westminster Standards and the 'Larger Hope'[1]

The doctrines of Calvinism formuiated in the Westminster Standards are represented by many persons as destining the vast majority of the human race to an eternity of sin and misery. They are pessimistic, it is said; enveloping this brief human life in gloom and darkness. The elect are very few; and the non-elect are very many. Practically, the human species is lost for ever, like the devil and his angels. Over this theological system they would write the Dantean inscription on the portal of Hell, 'All hope abandon, ye who enter here'. We shall endeavor to show that this estimate is utterly erroneous, and that 'the system of doctrine contained in the Scriptures', and presented in the Confession, teaches that an immense majority of the human family will be saved by the redemption of the dying and risen Son of God and Lord of Glory, and that the 'larger hope' has ample scope and verge enough within its limits.

Calvinism emphasizes the doctrine of *regeneration*: the doctrine, namely, that God by an instantaneous act imparts the principle of spiritual life to the sinful soul without its co-operation or assistance, so that the new birth is not dependent upon, or conditioned by, man's agency. Men who are 'born again' are 'born not of blood, nor of the will of the flesh, nor of the will of man, but of

---

[1] In part, from the Methodist Quarterly Review, May, 1889.

God' (*John 1: 13*). This doctrine runs all through the Westminster Standards. It is closely connected with the tenet of *election*, for this regulates the bestowment of regenerating grace. *Effectual calling* includes it, for a prominent factor in this is that work of God whereby he 'takes away the heart of stone, and gives the heart of flesh' (Conf. x. 1). In thus magnifying regeneration, the Confession accords with Revelation. For on looking into the Scriptures, we find that the salvation of the human soul is made to depend absolutely upon the new birth. Christ said to Nicodemus, 'Except a man be born again, he cannot see the kingdom of God'. This implies that every man who *is* born again will see the kingdom of God. Regeneration, consequently, decides human destiny. Whoever knows how many of the human family shall have been quickened from spiritual death to spiritual life, by the mercy of God the Holy Spirit, knows how many of them shall be saved. Regeneration determines human salvation, because it produces everything requisite to it. The great act of faith in the blood of Christ, by which the sinner is justified, is described as dependent upon it. 'Whosoever believeth that Jesus is the Christ, is born of God' (*I John 5: 1*). 'No man can come to me, except the Father which hath sent me draw him' (*John 6: 44*). 'Ye believed, even as the Lord gave to every man' (*I Cor. 3: 5*). 'As many as were ordained to eternal life believed' (*Acts 13: 48*). 'Unto you it is given in the behalf of Christ, to believe on him' (*Phil. 1: 29*). 'By grace are ye saved through faith; and that not of yourselves: it is the gift of God' (*Eph. 2: 8*). 'Christ is the author and finisher of faith' (*Heb. 12: 2*). Faith, repentance, justification, and sanctification all result naturally and infallibly from that work of the Holy Spirit, whereby he 'quickens' the soul 'dead in trespasses and sins' (*Eph. 2: 1*), and by 'enlightening the mind, and renewing the will, persuades and enables man to embrace Jesus Christ, freely offered to him in the gospel' (Shorter Catechism, 31). Regeneration is thus the root from which the whole process of salvation springs. The regenerate child, youth, or man, immediately believes, repents, and begins the struggle with remaining sin. The regenerate infant believes, repents, and begins the struggle with remaining sin the moment his faculties admit of such activities. He has *latent* or *potential* faith, repentance, and sanctification.

How *extensive* then is regeneration, is the great question. In Scripture and in the Confession it is represented to be as extensive as election, and no more so. 'Whom he did predestinate, them he also called; and whom he called, them he also justified; and whom he justified, them he also glorified' (*Rom. 8: 30*). 'All those whom God hath predestinated unto life, and those only, he is pleased, in his appointed and accepted time, effectually to call, by his word and Spirit, out of the state of sin and death, to grace and salvation by Jesus Christ' (Conf. x. 1). In attempting, therefore, to answer approximately that question which our Lord declined to answer definitely, namely, 'Are there few that be saved?' it is necessary, first, to determine the *period* within which the regenerating operation of the Holy Spirit occurs; and, secondly, the *range* of his operation.

Respecting the first point, revelation teaches that the new birth is confined to earth and time. There is not a passage in Scripture which, either directly or by implication, asserts that the Holy Ghost will exert his regenerating power in the soul of man in any part of that endless duration which succeeds this life. The affirmation, 'My Spirit shall not always strive with man' (*Gen. 6: 3*), proves that the dispensation of the Spirit will not be *everlasting*; and the accompanying declaration, 'Yet his days shall be a hundred and twenty years', implies that it will be coterminous with man's mortal life. Accordingly, in the

Old Testament, the death of the body is represented as the decisive epoch in man's existence, and this earthly life the period during which his endless destiny is determined. 'The wicked is driven away in his wickedness [at death]; but the righteous hath hope in his *death*' (*Prov. 14: 32*). 'When a wicked man *dieth*, his expectation shall perish' (*Prov. 11: 7*). 'If thou warn the wicked of his way to turn from it; if he do not turn from his way, he shall *die* in his iniquity' (*Ezek. 33: 9*). 'To him that is joined to all the living, there is hope: for the living know that they shall die; but the *dead* know not anything, neither have they any more a reward' (*Eccl. 9: 4–6*). 'In *death* there is no remembrance of thee; in the *grave*, who shall give thee thanks?' (*Ps. 6: 5*). 'Wilt thou show wonders to the *dead*? Shall the *dead* arise and praise thee? Shall thy loving-kindness be declared in the *grave*?' (*Ps. 88: 10, 11*). In the New Testament, the Saviour of man also makes death to be the critical point in man's history. He says to the Pharisees, 'If ye believe not that I am he, ye shall die in your sins' (*John 8: 21, 24*). This solemn warning, which he twice repeats, loses all its force, if to die in sin is not to be hopelessly lost. Christ teaches the same truth in the parable of Dives. The rich man asks that his brethren may be exhorted to faith and repentance before they *die*, because if impenitent at death as he was, they will go to 'hell' as he did, and be 'in torments' as he was. And he teaches the same truth in his frequent warning, 'Watch, therefore, for ye know not at what hour your Lord cometh' (*Matt. 24: 42*). The Apostolical Epistles declare the momentous nature of death, in their frequent assertion of 'an accepted time', and of 'the day of salvation' (*2 Cor. 6: 2; Heb. 3: 7–19; 4: 7*). The closing up of the Word of God by St. John, affirms a finality that evidently refers to what man has been and done here on earth. 'He that is unjust, let him be unjust still; and he which is filthy, let him be filthy still; and he that is righteous, let him be righteous still; and he that is holy, let him be holy still' (*Rev. 22: 11, 12*).

Still further proof that death is the deciding point in man's existence, is found in those *effects of regeneration* which have been spoken of. Faith, repentance, hope, and struggle with remaining sin are never represented in Scripture as occurring in the future life. After death the regenerate walks by sight, not by faith; has fruition instead of hope; and is completely sanctified. Faith, repentance, hope, and progressive sanctification are described as going on up to a certain point denominated 'the *end*', when they give place to sinless perfection. 'He that endureth to the end shall be saved': the end of this state of existence, not of the intermediate state. 'We desire that every one of you do show the same diligence to the full assurance of hope unto the end.' 'Christ shall confirm you unto the end.' 'Whose house are we, if we hold fast the confidence and the rejoicing of the hope unto the end.' In all such passages, the end of this mortal life is meant. And to them must be added the important eschatological paragraph, I Cor. 15: 24–28, which teaches that there is an 'end' to Christ's work of mediation and salvation, when 'there remaineth no more sacrifice for sins' (*Heb. 10: 26*).

The large amount of matter in Scripture which teaches that the operation of the Spirit in the new birth and its effects belongs only to this life, cannot be invalidated by the lonely text concerning Christ's 'preaching to the spirits in prison': a passage which the majority of exegetes, taking in all ages of the Church, refer to the preaching of Noah and other 'ambassadors of Christ'; but which, even if referred to a personal descent of Christ into an under world, would be inadequate to establish such a revolutionizing doctrine as the prolongation of Christ's mediatorial work into the future stage, the preaching of the gospel in sheol, and the outpouring of the Holy Ghost there. For the dogma of a future redemption for all the unevangelized part of mankind is radically revolutionizing. It is another gospel, and if adopted would result in another Christendom. For nearly twenty centuries, the Church has gone upon the belief that there is no salvation after death. All of its conquests over evil have come from preaching the solemn truth that 'now is the day of salvation'. It has believed itself to be commanded to proclaim that 'after death is the *judgment*' of sin, not its forgiveness. But if the Church has been mistaken, and there is a 'probation' in the future life for all the unevangelized of all the centuries, and it is announced, as all the truth of God ought to be, then the eternal world will present a totally different aspect from what it has. Heretofore the great Hereafter has been a gulf of darkness for every impenitent man, heathen or nominal Christian, as he peered into it. Now it will be a darkness through which gleams of light and hope are flashing like an aurora. The line between time and eternity, so sharply drawn by the past Christianity and Christendom, must be erased. A different preaching must be adopted. Hope must be held out instead of the old hopelessness. Death must no longer be represented as a finality, but as an entrance for all unevangelized mankind upon another period of regeneration and salvation. Men must be told that the Semiramises and Cleopatras, the Tiberiuses and Neros, may possibly have accepted the gospel in hades. Children in the Sabbath-schools must be taught that the vicious and hardened populations of the ancient world, of Sodom and Gomorrah, of Babylon and Nineveh, of Antioch and Rome, passed into a world of hope and redemption, not of justice and judgment.

Such a doctrine takes away all the seriousness of this existence. The 'threescore years and ten' are no longer momentous in their consequences. If the future world is a series of cycles, within any one of which the transition from sin to holiness, from death to life, may occur, all the solemnity is removed from earth and time. The 'now' is not 'the accepted time, and the day of salvation'. One 'time' is of no more consequence than another, if through all endless time the redemption of sinners is going on. And what is still more important, the moral and practical effects of this theory will be most disastrous. For it is virtually a *license to sin*. Should God announce that he will regenerate and pardon men in the next world, it would be equivalent to saying to them that they may continue to sin in this world. And, of course, if the Church should believe that all the unevangelized portion of mankind may be saved in the intermediate state, it will make little effort to save them here and now.

With these representations of Scripture, respecting the period of time within which the regeneration and salvation of the soul occur, the Westminster Standards agree. 'The souls of believers are at their *death* made perfect in holiness, and do immediately pass into glory' (S.C. 37). 'The souls of the wicked are at their *death* cast into hell' (L.C. 86). The Confessional doctrine is, that death is a finality for both the saint and sinner. There is no extirpation of sin after 'the spirit returns to God who gave it'. At death, the unregenerate man is left in sin. At death, the regenerate but imperfectly sanctified man is made perfect in holiness. The gradual process of progressive sanctification from the remainders of original corruption, is confined to this life. So the Scriptures teach. 'Blessed are the dead that die in the Lord from henceforth [i.e., from the time of their death]: Yea, saith the Spirit, that they may *rest* from their labors' (*Rev. 14: 13*). 'There remaineth a *rest* to the people of God. Let us therefore labor to enter into that *rest* (*Heb. 4: 9, 11*). This 'rest' is total cessation from the temptation, the race, and the fight with sin which characterize the present imperfect state. 'To be absent from the body, is to be present with the Lord' (*2 Cor. 5: 8*); and to be present with the Lord is to 'see him as he is'; and to see him as he is, is to 'be like him', sinless and perfect (*I John 3: 2*).

The doctrine that gradual sanctification from sin continues to go on after death implies, not rest, but struggle, strain, toil, and conflict with remaining corruption. This would be a continuation in the next life of that severe experience in this life in which the believer 'groans, being burdened'; in which he is often worsted in the contest, though victorious in the main; in which he cries, 'O wretched man, who shall deliver me'. To suppose such a wearisome condition of the believer's soul during the long period between death and the resurrection, cannot be harmonized with the descriptions of the restful, joyful consciousness of believers when they are 'with the Lord', and with the words of Christ, 'This day shalt thou be with me in paradise'.

The notion that indwelling sin is to be purged away gradually after death, instead of instantaneously at death, is the substance of the doctrine of purgatory. The Romish purgatory is the progressive sanctification of a member of the Romish Church carried over into the intermediate state. If this theory is introduced into the Protestant Church, it will not stop here. For if regenerate but imperfectly sanctified men are to go on, between death and the resurrection, struggling with corruption, and getting rid of remaining sin, as they do here upon earth, it will be an easy and natural step to the kindred theory that the transition from sin to holiness may be made by *unregenerate* men also during this same period. Those who adopt this latter error, object to the Confessional tenet of complete sanctification at death by the immediate operation of the Holy Spirit that it is magical, mechanical, and unpsychological. It is incompatible, they assert, with the spiritual nature of the soul and its free agency. But it is no more so than the co-ordinate and cognate doctrine of the immediate operation of the Holy Spirit in regeneration. The Holy Spirit *instantaneously* implants the new principle of divine life in the soul, when he 'creates it anew in Christ Jesus', and 'quickens it from its death in trespasses and sins'. This lays the foundation, as we have observed, for the whole process of salvation. From this instantaneous regeneration, there result conversion in its two acts of faith and repentance, justification, and progressive sanctification up to the moment of death, when the same Divine Agent by the exercise of the same almighty energy by which he instantaneously began the work of salvation, instantaneously completes it.[1] Now, if the Holy Ghost works magically, mechanically, and contrary to the nature of the human soul in one case, he does in the other. If the completion of the work in the soul by an immediate act is liable to this charge, the beginning of it is also. Any one who holds the doctrine of instantaneous regeneration, is stopped from urging such an objection as this to the doctrine of complete sanctification at death. In all the operations of the third Person of the Trinity, be they instantaneous or be they gradual, he contradicts none of the laws and properties of the human mind, but works in the human will 'to will', according to its nature and constitution. There is nothing magical, mechanical, or unpsychological in any of them.

Another objection urged by the advocates of a future sanctification from sin is, that complete sanctification at death puts all souls, infant and adult, on a dead level, destroying the distinction of grade between them. If at death all regenerate souls are made perfectly sinless and

[1] For a fuller discussion of the subject, see the Author's Sermons to the Spiritual Man, pp. 317–325.

holy, it is said that they must be all alike in the scope and reach of their faculties. This does not follow. Complete sanctification at death frees the soul of a regenerate infant from all remainders of the corruption inherited from Adam, but does not convert it into an adult soul, any more than the complete sanctification of an ordinary regenerate adult makes him equal in mental power to St. Paul or St. Augustine. Complete sanctification at death frees the infant's soul, the child's soul, the youth's soul, the man's soul, from indwelling sin, but leaves each soul in the same class in which it finds it, and starts it on an endless expansion of its faculties and its holiness, and not upon a long, wearing struggle with remaining corruption. In this way, 'one star differeth from another star in glory', while all are equally and alike the pure and gleaming stars of heaven, not the 'wandering stars' of sin and hell.

Such, then, is the *period* of time to which the regenerating work of the Holy Spirit is confined. It is the life that now is, not the life that is to come; the present limited æon, not the future unlimited æon. We proceed now to consider the second question, How *wide* and *extensive* is his agency during this period? How many of the human family, have we reason from Scripture to hope and believe, he will regenerate here upon earth?

Before proceeding to answer this question, a preliminary remark is to be made. It is utterly improbable that such a stupendous miracle as the incarnation, humiliation, passion, and crucifixion of one of the Persons of the Godhead, should yield a small and insignificant result; that this amazing mystery of mysteries, 'which the angels desire to look into', and which involves such an immense personal sacrifice on the part of the Supreme Being, should have a lame and impotent conclusion. On a priori grounds, therefore, we have reason to conclude that the Gospel of the Cross will be successful, and the Christian

[125]

religion a triumph on the earth and among the race of creatures for whom it was intended. But this can hardly be the case, if only a small fraction of the human family are saved. The presumption, consequently, is that the great majority of mankind, not the small minority of it, will be the subjects of redeeming grace. What, then, is the teaching of Revelation upon this subject?

1. In the first place, we have ground for believing that all of mankind who die in infancy will be regenerated by the Holy Spirit. The proof of this is not so abundant as for some other doctrines, but it is sufficient for faith. (a) Scripture certainly teaches that the children of the regenerate are 'bound up in the bundle of life' with their parents. 'The promise [of the Holy Spirit] is unto you and your children' (*Acts 2: 38, 39*). 'If the root be holy, so are the branches' (*Rom. 11: 16*). 'The unbelieving husband is sanctified by the wife, and the unbelieving wife is sanctified by the husband: else were your children unclean, but now they are holy' (*I Cor. 7: 14*). This is salvation by covenanted mercy, concerning which there is little dispute. (b) The salvation of infants outside of the covenant, is plainly supported by the language of Christ respecting 'little children' as a *special class*. 'They brought unto him infants that he would touch them. And he said, Suffer little children to come unto me, for of such is the kingdom of God' (*Luke 18: 15, 16*). The reason here assigned why infants constitute a part of the kingdom of God is their *infancy*, not their moral character. They belong to it solely because they are 'little children', not because they are sinless. Our Lord teaches that they are sinful, in saying, 'Suffer little children to come unto me'; for no sinless beings need to come to a Saviour. This phraseology respecting infants is as all-inclusive as that respecting the 'poor in spirit', and cannot be restricted to a part of them. When Christ says, 'Blessed are the poor in

spirit, for theirs is the kingdom of heaven', he means that this kingdom belongs to them *as* poor in spirit, and *because* they are poor in spirit, and consequently belongs to *all* the poor in spirit. And, similarly, when he says, 'Suffer little children to come unto me, for of such is the kingdom of God', he means that this kingdom is composed of such considered *as* little children, and *because* they are little children, and consequently is composed of *all* the little children. Had he intended to limit his statement to some infants, he would have said, ἐκ τῶν τοιούτων ἐστίν. Infancy is an age that is singled out by the Saviour by which to prove a membership in the kingdom of God from the *very age itself*, and is the only age. He does not say that youths or adults constitute a part of the kingdom of God solely because of their youth, or their manhood. Other Scripture proofs of the salvation of infants are, Matt. 18: 10, 14, 'Their angels do always behold the face of my Father in heaven. It is not the will of your Father which is in heaven that one of these little ones should perish'. In 2 Sam. 12: 23, David is confident of the salvation of his infant child; but in 2 Sam. 18: 33, he is not confident of the salvation of his adult son. In Jonah 4: 11, God expresses a special interest in the infant population of Nineveh.

The Protestant Church understands the Bible to declare that all who die in infancy die regenerate. Probably all evangelical denominations, without committing themselves to the statements of the Westminster Confession concerning 'election', would be willing to say that all dying infants 'are regenerated and saved by Christ through the Spirit, who worketh when, and where, and how he pleaseth' (Conf. x. 3). But this is the regeneration and salvation of one-half of the human family. This of itself pours over human existence a mild and cheering light. 'Whom the gods love, die young', said the heathen, without any knowledge of God's compassion for man in his 'dear Son'. Much more, then, may the Christian under the irradiation of the gospel expect that the infinite mercy of God, by 'the washing of regeneration and renewing of the Holy Ghost', will bring all the 'little children' into holiness and heaven. The gloom of Virgil's description,

> Continuo auditæ voces, vagitus et ingens
> Infantumque animæ flentes in limine primo,

is changed into the brightness of that of the prophet, 'The streets of the city shall be full of boys and girls playing in the streets thereof' (*Zech. 8: 10*); and of the Redeemer's citation from the Psalms, 'Out of the mouth of babes and sucklings thou hast perfected praise' (*Matt. 21: 16*).

2. In the second place, the Scriptures and the Confession teach the regeneration of a vast multitude, from Adam down, who come under the operation of the Holy Spirit in connection with the special revelation and the external means of grace, in the antediluvian, patriarchal, Jewish, and Christian Churches.

3. In the third place, the Scriptures and the Confession teach that the Divine Spirit exerts his regenerating grace, to some extent, within adult heathendom, making use of conscience, or 'the law written on the heart', as the means of convicting of sin preparatory to imparting the new divine life; and that in the last day a part of God's elect 'shall come from the east and from the west, and from the north and from the south, and shall sit down in the kingdom of God' (*Luke 13: 29*). These are all regenerated in this life. And since regeneration in the instance of the adult immediately produces faith and repentance, a regenerate heathen is both a believer and a penitent. He feels sorrow for sin, and the need of mercy. This felt need of mercy and desire for it is potentially and virtually faith in the Redeemer. For although the Redeemer has not been presented to him historically and personally as the object

of faith, yet the Divine Spirit by the new birth has wrought in him the sincere and longing *disposition* to believe in him. With the penitent and believing man in the Gospel, he says, 'Who is he, Lord, that I might believe on him?' (*John 9: 36*). Such a man is 'regenerated and saved by Christ through the Spirit', and belongs to that class of 'elect persons who are incapable of being outwardly called by the ministry of the word' (Conf. x. 3).

4. In the fourth place, in addition to all this work of the Holy Spirit in the past and present in applying in these three ways the redemption that is in Christ Jesus, there is that mightiest and most wonderful manifestation of his power which is still in reserve for the future of Christendom. The Scriptures promise an outpouring in the 'last days', that will far exceed in sweeping and irresistible energy anything in the past history of the Church. 'I will pour out my Spirit upon all flesh', says God (Joel 2: 28). 'It shall come to pass in the last days, that the mountain of the Lord's house shall be established in the top of the mountains, and shall be exalted above the hills, and all nations shall flow unto it' (*Isa. 2: 2; Micah 4: 1*). A far more profound and all-reaching interest in the concerns of the soul and its eternal destiny than has ever been witnessed on earth, will mark the millennium. The then near and impending advent of the Son of man, 'when he shall come in his glory, and all the holy angels with him, and before him shall be gathered all nations' (*Matt. 25: 31, 32*), will weigh heavily upon mankind. The end of the world and the approaching judgment will be facts of infinite meaning. This human life, now so frivolous, will become serious and awful.

> The clouds that gather round the *setting* sun
> Do take a sober coloring from the eye
> That doth keep watch o'er man's *mortality*.

Vast masses of sinful men will be bowed down in poignant conviction, and nations will be born in a day. The Redeemer, 'travelling in the greatness of his strength', will take unto him his mighty power, and turn the human heart as the rivers of water. Such is the promise and the prophecy of Almighty God.

Now *this is a great salvation*. 'Where sin abounded, grace has superabounded' (*Rom. 5: 20*). The immense majority of the race that fell in Adam will be saved in Christ, 'by the washing of regeneration'. Though some men and angels will freely persist in depravity, and be left in their persistence, yet this minor and mournful note of discord will only enhance the choral harmony of the universe. The wrath of man shall praise God (*Ps. 76: 10*). The duty of the Church is to preach to every creature the *law* by which men are convicted of sin, and the *gospel* by which it is pardoned and eradicated, praying unceasingly for the outpouring of the Holy Ghost, to make both law and gospel effectual to salvation. Instead of starting a false and delusive hope for the future redemption of a part of the human family, by daring to reconstruct God's plan of redemption and extending the dispensation of his Spirit into the next life, the Church should strengthen the old and true hope by doing with its might what its hands find to do, and crying with the evangelical prophet, 'Awake, awake, put on strength, O arm of the Lord' (*Isa. 51: 9*).[1]

[1] It should be observed that the 'larger hope' that the Divine Mercy may save a part of the unevangelized millions of mankind does not require the extension of the work of redemption beyond this life. The 'washing of regeneration and renewing of the Holy Ghost' can accomplish this salvation here in this world, before the spirit leaves the body and 'returns to God who gave it', as easily as it can in the middle state. Instead, then, of hoping that there may be a second period of redemption, for which there is no more Scripture foundation than for a second incarnation, let the hope rather be that the merciful Redeemer, who is 'mighty to save', may here, and in this 'day of salvation', save a part of the heathen world. He himself asserts his

own sovereignty in this matter, and declares that some whose outward circumstances were favorable to salvation will be lost, and that some whose outward circumstances were unfavorable will be saved. 'There shall be weeping and gnashing of teeth, when ye shall see Abraham, and Isaac, and Jacob, and all the prophets in the kingdom of God, and you yourselves cast out. And they shall come from the east, and from the west, and from the north, and from the south, and shall sit down in the kingdom of God. And behold, there are last which shall be first, and there are first which shall be last' (*Luke 13: 28–30*).

13: The Westminster Affirmation of the Original Inerrancy of the Scriptures

Those who deny the inerrancy of the original autographs of Scripture, and are endeavoring to introduce this view into Biblical Criticism, claim the support of the Westminster Standards. We propose to show that the Westminster Confession teaches that the Scriptures in their first form, as they came from the prophets and apostles, were free from error in all their parts, secondary as well as primary.

1. In the first place, the Confession (i. 2, 8) declares that 'the Word of God as written in Hebrew and Greek was immediately inspired by God'. This relates to the *autographs* of the 'holy men of God' while under the Divine afflatus or inbreathing. 2 Pet. 1: 21. And it relates to them in their entirety, because no exceptions are made. The inspiration was plenary, not partial. It extended not to one subject only, but to all the subjects of which the sacred writers treat, and on which they profess to teach the truth. The history, chronology, topography, and physics, as well as the theology and ethics, that were composed under the 'immediate inspiration' of God, must from the nature of the case have been free from error. In the original Bible as it came from the inspired prophets and apostles, there was no mythical and fabulous history, no exaggerated and fictitious chronology like that of Egypt, India, and some modern physicists, the topography was strikingly accurate as modern explorations show, and the physics, especially in the account of the creative days, contained

none of the pantheism and polytheism of the ancient cosmogonies, and is corroborated by modern science so far as this is well established. In thus declaring that the Bible as a complete whole was written in Hebrew and Greek by persons who were under the 'immediate inspiration' of God, the Confession teaches that in this first original form it was inerrant. There is no escaping this conclusion, unless it can be shown that immediate inspiration may be more or less erroneous and misleading.

2. In the second place, the Confession (i. 8) declares that 'the Old Testament in Hebrew and the New Testament in Greek, being immediately inspired by God, is by his singular care and providence kept pure in all ages, and is therefore authentical [*i.e.* authoritative], so that in all controversies of religion the church is finally to appeal to them'. This relates to the *copies* of the original autographs. The Confession does not say that these were made under the 'immediate inspiration' of God as the autographs were, but under the 'singular care and providence' of God. The copies consequently are liable to the introduction of errors, because the providential care of God, even though it be 'singular' and remarkable, is not the same thing as the 'immediate inspiration' of God. While, therefore, absolute inerrancy is attributed by the Confession to the original manuscript, it is not to the copies of them. The immediate inspiration of a prophet or apostle, extending as the Confession declares to the Word as *written*, excludes all error from the written production, but the providential superintendence of a copyist does not. God has permitted some things in the providential transmission and preservation of the several books of Scripture, which he did not permit in the direct inspiration of them. He has allowed glosses on the margin to get into the text, numerals represented by letters of the alphabet to be altered by carelessness, a frequent cause of discrepancies

in the Old Testament, clauses to be omitted from homœoteleuton,[1] or added by paraphrase or from ancient liturgies, and other variations of this kind. But he did not allow any of these variations and errors to get into the original writing, as it came from the inspired penman who composed it. And there is no reason, in the nature of the case, for asserting that he did. Does it follow that because the existing copies of 1 Sam. 6: 19 contain the statement that 50,070 men were slain for looking into the ark, that the autograph also did? Because the copies of the autographs of the New Testament contain 30,000 variations according to Mill, and 150,000 according to Scrivener, must we assume that the autographs themselves had all these, or any of them?

But while the Confession ascribes providential superintendence, not immediate inspiration, to the copyist, it claims for all copies of the autographs a relative in distinction from an absolute inerrancy. The 'singular care and providence of God keeps them pure in all ages so that they are authentical', that is, authoritative, and 'in all controversies of religion, the church is finally to appeal to them'. Con. i. 8. The minor and unimportant errors of the class above mentioned, which have been allowed by Divine providence to get into the copies, do not make any *radical* and *essential* alterations in the autographs. A student of the copy today will obtain from it the same doctrine, the same history, the same chronology, the same topography, and the same physics, that he would from the original autograph if he could have access to it. The doctrines of the Trinity, the incarnation, the apostasy, and the redemption, are confessedly unaffected by any of these variations in the history or topography. And the

[1] The technical term for the error of a copyist when similar endings to two lines or statements cause confusion in transcription, resulting in the omission of the material in between.

Biblical chronology itself is not essentially altered by the numerical errors which the carelessness of the copist has introduced. For example, the contradiction between 2 Kings 8: 26 and 2 Chron. 22: 2, in the existing manuscripts, does not invalidate the chronology of the fifth and the eleventh chapters of Genesis. There is nothing in any of the alleged or the actual chronological mistakes in any of the copies of the Scriptures, that necessitates the rejection of the Biblical chronology which brings the whole of human history before the Advent within a period of four or six thousand years, according as the Hebrew or the Septuagint text is adopted. And this remark applies also to the *versions* of Scripture which have been and will be made by the Church. These convey to the nations of mankind the same doctrine, history, chronology, topography, and physics that were taught by the prophets and apostles, although they contain some errors in translation.

The question is asked in the way of objection to this declaration of the Confession, Why did not God inspire the copyists as well as the original authors? Why did he begin with absolute inerrancy, and end with relative inerrancy? For the same reason that, generally, he begins with the supernatural and ends with the natural. For illustration, the first founding of his church, in both the Old and New dispensations, was marked by miracles; but the development of it is marked only by his operations in nature, providence, and grace. The miracle was needed in order to *begin* the kingdom of God in this sinful world, but is not needed in order to its continuance and progress. And the same is true of the revelation of God in his written Word. This must *begin* in a miracle. The truths and facts of revealed religion, as distinguished from natural, must be supernaturally communicated to a few particular persons especially chosen for this purpose. Inspiration comes under the category of the miracle. It is as miraculous as raising the dead. To expect, therefore, that God would continue inspiration to copyists after having given it to prophets and apostles, would be like expecting that because in the first century he empowered men to raise the dead, he would continue to do so in all centuries. If this had been necessary, if God could not have extended and perpetuated his church without the continuance of miracles, doubtless he would have wrought miracles perpetually; for we can not suppose that Omnipotence would suffer itself to be defeated in any undertaking. But whatever can be accomplished by his ordinary methods in nature, providence, and grace, God so accomplishes.

Now, this applies to divine revelation. The Scriptures could not have been originated and written down in the vernacular of the prophets and apostles without an inerrant and infallible inspiration, and as thus originated and written they were perfect, containing no error. God the Holy Spirit inspires no error, great or small. This is miracle. But these Scriptures can be copied into thousands of manuscripts, so that these shall substantially reproduce the autographs in doctrine, history, physics, chronology, geography; in short, in everything that goes to make up the Scriptures. This latter process is not supernatural and preclusive of all error, but providential and natural and allowing of some error. But this substantial reproduction, this relative 'purity' of the original text as copied, is sufficient for the Divine purposes in carrying forward the work of redemption in the world. But had the employment of this method of special providence involved the radical alteration of the original autographs, so as to introduce essential and fatal error into them, then doubtless it would not have been employed, but the copyists as well as the prophets and apostles would have been supernaturally 'moved by the Holy Ghost', and their copies would have been exact *fac-similes* of the autographs.

One or the other view of the Scriptures must be adopted; either that they were originally inerrant and infallible, or that they were originally errant and fallible. The first view is that of the church in all ages: the last is that of the rationalist in all ages. He who adopts the first view, will naturally bend all his efforts to eliminate the errors of copyists and harmonize discrepancies, and thereby bring the existing manuscripts nearer to the original autographs. By this process, the errors and discrepancies gradually diminish, and belief in the infallibility of Scripture is strengthened. He who adopts the second view, will naturally bend all his efforts to perpetuate the mistakes of scribes, and exaggerate and establish discrepancies. By this process, the errors and discrepancies gradually increase, and disbelief in the infallibility of Scripture is strengthened. That the theory of the original errancy and fallibility of Scripture as it came from the prophets and apostles should be maintained and defended by the rationalistic critic, is comprehensible – his hostility to the supernatural explains it – but that it should be maintained and defended by professedly evangelical critics, is inexplicable, except on the supposition that they do not perceive the logical result of the theory, and its exceedingly destructive influence upon the belief of mankind in Divine Revelation.

Nearly forty years ago, the author, in criticizing the theory strongly and eloquently presented by Coleridge in his Confessions of an Inquiring Spirit, that the secondary sections of Scripture contain more or less of error, while the primary section relating to doctrine is inerrant, made the following objections to it, which he has seen no reason to modify. 'We are aware that Coleridge believed that the Scriptures are infallible on all fundamental subjects, and that those doctrines which in common with the Christian Church he regarded as vital to human salvation, are all infallibly revealed in them. This separates him heaven-wide from a mere rationalist, and places him in the same general class with the evangelical school of theologians in Germany, in respect to the doctrine of inspiration. Still, we regard it as an error in him and in them, that the canon is not contemplated as a complete *whole*, having a *common* origin in the Divine Mind, in such sense that as a body of information it is infallibly correct on all the subjects upon which it purports to teach truth. There must be truth, in distinction from error, upon even the most unimportant particulars of history, chronology, topography, and physics constituting a part of the subject-matter of the Bible, and it is altogether the most rational to assume that it is to be found in the Biblical statements themselves if they are inspired of God. These secondary subjects are an important, and sometimes a vital part of the total Word of God. The biographic memoirs of the Redeemer are an instance. If these are not inerrant as history and chronology, then the Christian religion itself disappears; for the Personage in whom it centres becomes mythical, instead of historic. Hence in the contest between rationalism and supernaturalism, the narratives in the four Gospels have been the hottest part of the battlefield. Consider again the long and detailed narratives of the exodus of the Israelites, and their wanderings for forty years. If these were not the inspired product of their leader and law-giver, but the compilation and invention of unknown persons living a thousand years after Moses, and in an environment wholly different from that of Egypt and the Sinaitic peninsula, this fictitious secondary matter will drag the primary along with it. Mankind will not believe that the theology and ethics of the decalogue, the sacrifices, types, and symbols of the Levitical institute, and the religion of the theocracy, came supernaturally from God, if they are imbedded in a mythical history and chronology like that of Egypt and

India. The secondary sections of which we are speaking, are so integrated into the solid doctrinal substance of the Bible, that they cannot be taken out of it any more than the veins can be from the solid marble. Why then is it not probable that they had the same common origin with the doctrines and fundamental truths themselves which are encrusted and crystallized in them – in other words, that the Divine Spirit, whether as positively revealing, or as inspiring and superintending, is the ultimate Author of the whole? There are but two objections to this position. The first is, that the inspired writers become thereby mere amanuenses and automata. This objection has no force for one who believes that the Divine can, and does dwell and work in the human in the most real and absolute manner, without in the least mutilating or suppressing the human, and ought not to be urged by one who believes in the actuation of the regenerate soul by the Holy Spirit. As in this instance the human cannot be separated from the Divine, in the individual consciousness, and all 'the fruits of the Spirit' seem to be the very spontaneity of the human soul itself, so in the origination of the entire body of Holy Writ, while all, even the minutest parts, have the flexibility, naturalness, and freshness of purely human products, there is yet in and through them all the unerring agency of the Supreme Mind. In other words, the Holy Spirit is the organizing power and principle in the outstanding body of knowledge and information which is called the Bible, and, working like every organizing power *thoroughly* and *completely*, produces a whole that is characterized by His own characteristic perfection of knowledge, even as the principle of life in the natural world diffuses itself, and produces all the characteristic marks of life, out to the rim of the tiniest leaf. The second objection, and a fatal one if it can be maintained, is, that there are actual errors in the Scriptures on points respecting which they profess to teach the truth. Let this be proved if it can be; but until it has been demonstrated incontrovertibly, the Christian Church is consistent in asserting the infallibility of the written Word in all its elements and parts. We say this with confidence, because out of the large number of alleged errors and contradictions that have been urged against the plenary inspiration of the Scriptures, by sceptics of all grades from Celsus and Porphyry down to Spinoza and Strauss, none are established as such on grounds that make it absurd for the defender of the doctrine to deny the allegation, and attempt an explanation and reconciliation of the difficulty. There are many perplexities remaining, we grant, but while there is not an instance in which the unprejudiced and truly scientific study of the Bible has resulted in demonstrating beyond dispute that an inspired prophet or apostle has taught error of any kind, there are many instances in which it has resulted in favor of plenary inspiration. No one acquainted with the results of the severe and sceptical criticism to which the canon has been subjected by the English deists of the eighteenth century, and the German rationalists of the nineteenth, will deny that the number of apparent contradictions and errors is smaller now than at the beginning of the controversy, and that the Divine origin and authority of the Old and New Testaments are resting on broader, deeper, and firmer foundations than ever'. Shedd: Literary Essays, 337–340.

Those who deny the inerrancy of the original autographs of the Scriptures are also chargeable with another misunderstanding of the Confession. They confound 'the testimony of any man or church' spoken of in Con. i. 4, with 'the testimony of the church' spoken of in Con. i. 5. In endeavoring, contrary to all the Christian apologetics of the past, to sever entirely the inspiration of the Scriptures from their authorship and authenticity, and to make belief in them depend solely upon the inward witness of the Spirit, thereby abolishing historical faith and retaining only saving faith, they argue that the exclusion of 'the testimony of any man or church' spoken of in Con. i. 4, excludes 'the testimony of the church' spoken of in Con. i. 5, and cite the former to show that the external evidence for the authenticity of Scripture which comes from the tradition of the Jewish and early Christian churches is not needed in order to prove its inspiration, or to strengthen confidence in it. In so doing they confound *authority* with *authenticity*, and overlook the two different uses of the term 'testimony' in the Confession. In Con. i. 4, the authority of the Scripture is spoken of, and the 'testimony' meant is testimony to the truth. In Con. i. 5, the authenticity of Scripture is spoken of, and the 'testimony' meant is testimony to the authorship and genuineness of a writing. An examination of the two sections will show this.

Con. i. 4 declares that 'the *authority* of Scripture dependeth not upon the testimony of any man or church, but wholly upon God, who is the author of it'. 'Testimony,' here, is used in the sense of teaching, declaring and communicating truth. The proof text cited from 1 John 5: 9 evinces this: 'If we receive the witness of men, the witness of God is greater'. To which may be added, with many another passage, John 5: 32, 34: 'I receive not testimony from men; there is another that beareth witness of me, and I know that the witness which he witnesseth of me is true'. Truth which God testifies to and so is the *author* of, has infallible authority; but truth which 'any man or church' testifies to and so is the *author* of, is fallible.

Con. i. 5 declares that 'we may be induced by the testimony of the church to a high and reverent esteem for the Holy Scriptures'. This relates to the *authenticity* of the

Bible; namely, to the fact of its being the genuine product of those inspired prophets and apostles through whom God 'testified' in the sense of Con. i. 4, and made his revelation of truth, in distinction from being the forged product of unknown men outside of the circle of prophets and apostles, writing centuries later. The 'testimony' spoken of in this section is not the teaching, declaring, and communicating of divine truth, but merely bearing witness that such and such persons wrote such and such parts of Scripture. The Jewish and early Christian churches, in rendering this important service, whereby the genuineness of the sacred writings is established by the same kind of testimony by which that of secular writings is proved, did not claim to be the *authors* of the Bible, or that it got its *authority* from them, but only to know that certain men who gave evidence by visible miraculous signs of being called and inspired of God wrote certain books of Scripture. Such external testimony as this to the genuineness of Scripture, supported by the infinitely higher testimony of Christ to the same effect in regard to the Old Testament, is as necessary in order to faith in it as a divine book as is the external testimony of the early Christian church that Christ and his apostles wrought miracles, in order to believe in miracles. Take away from Christendom the external evidence which the 'eye-witnesses' (*2 Pet. 1: 16*) and contemporaries of our Lord and his apostles gave to miracles, and belief in miracles would soon yield to sceptical attacks. The internal evidence alone would not save it. Take away from Christendom the testimony which contemporaries have given that the four Gospels were the productions of the four Evangelists, and belief in their infallible inspiration would soon die out. The internal evidence alone would not be sufficient to keep the faith of the church firm, after the invalidation of their genuineness and canonicity. We already see the mischievous effect of even the defeated attempt to destroy the force of the early ecclesiastical testimony and catholic tradition respecting the authorship of the Gospels, in lessening confidence in them as inspired narratives.

And the reason is, that inspiration from the nature of the case belongs only to a very small circle, and not to mankind generally, nor to a nation generally. A book, in order to be inspired, *must originate within this very small circle.* Hence the question of authorship is inseparable from that of inspiration. Whoever could prove indisputably that Matthew's gospel was not written by or under the superintendence of one of 'those men which companied with the Lord Jesus all the time that he went in and out' on earth (*Acts 1: 21*), and whom he set apart and endowed with both inspiration and miraculous powers, in order to found his church and prepare an authoritative account of his life and teachings for Christendom in all time – whoever could indisputably prove that it was written by some unknown person in the second century who never saw Christ on earth and had no personal connection with him of any kind, would prove that it was a forgery and destroy human confidence in it. And this confidence would not be restored by merely saying, 'The first Gospel was not written by Matthew, but whoever it was that wrote it he was inspired'. For this makes the inspiration depend upon the testimony of the modern individual who says so, instead of the testimony of the Primitive church. The only sponsor for the inspiration of an 'unknown man' is the unknown man that asserts such an inspiration.

Both the external and internal evidences for the inspiration of the Scriptures are necessary; and so are both historical and saving faith. A man who is destitute of the former is never the subject of the latter; the former is a preparative to the latter. Sceptics, remaining such, are never converted. Consequently God provides the external

[143]

evidence which produces historical faith, as well as the inward operation of the Holy Spirit which produces saving faith. There is no need of undervaluing the very great strength of the internal evidence while insisting upon the full value of the external. Inspiration is a *supernatural* fact, like miracles; and, as we cannot rely wholly upon the internal evidence for a miracle, upon its intrinsic nature and probability, but must bring in the external evidence, namely, the actual seeing of it by an eyewitness, so in the case of inspiration, in addition to the nature of the truths taught and the probability that a benevolent and paternal Being would make some communications to his creatures respecting their origin and eternal destiny, we must add that which comes from the testimony of those who lived contemporaneously with prophets and apostles respecting their right to be regarded as the authors of the writings attributed to them, and the supernatural evidences which they gave that they were under a divine afflatus, and were the 'holy men of God, who spake as they were moved by the Holy Ghost'.

14: *Calvinism and the Bible*

The question, What is the system of doctrine contained in the Westminster Confession, and what is essential to its integrity? is more important than ever, now that the Presbyteries have voted in favor of revision, and the General Assembly has instructed its committee 'not to propose any alterations or amendments that will in any way impair the integrity of the Reformed or Calvinistic system of doctrine taught in the Confession of Faith'. The vote of the Church in answer to the overture of the fifteen Presbyteries shows that sixty-eight Presbyteries desire no revision at all of their Standards, and that ninety-two desire no revision that would alter the doctrinal system contained in them. This vote evinces that at least three-fourths of the Northern Presbyterian Church wish to be known as a Calvinistic denomination, in distinction from a Broad Church, tolerating all varieties of 'evangelical' belief; and the general tenor of the discussion in the late Assembly was strongly against the dis-Calvinizing of the Confession.

Some advocates of revision object to this decision of the Assembly to make Calvinism a test of revision, and demand that Scripture be the test. Of course Scripture is the only infallible rule of faith. But this particular way of appealing to Scripture is specious and fallacious. In the first place, it assumes that Calvinism is not Scriptural, an assumption which the Presbyterian Church has never granted. This Church does not accept the alternative – the

Bible *or* Calvinism – presented in this appeal. Its watch-word, is The Bible *and* Calvinism. Secondly, this kind of appeal to Scripture is only an appeal to Scripture as the reviser understands it. 'Scripture' properly means the interpretation of Scripture; that is, the contents of Scripture as reached by human investigation and exegesis. Creeds, like commentaries, are Scripture studied and explained, and not the mere abstract and unexplained book as it lies on the counter of the Bible House. The infallible Word of God is expounded by the fallible mind of man, and hence the variety of expositions embodied in the denominational creeds. But every interpreter claims to have understood the Scriptures correctly, and, consequently, claims that his creed is Scriptural, and if so, that it is the infallible truth of God. The Arminian appeals to the Articles of Wesley as the rule of faith, because he believes them to be the true explanation of the inspired Bible. For him they are the Bible in a nutshell. The Calvinist appeals to the creeds of Heidelberg, Dort, and Westminster as the rule of faith, because he regards them as the accurate exegesis of the revealed Word of God. By the 'Bible' these parties, as well as all others who appeal to the Bible, mean their understanding of the Bible. There is no such thing as that abstract Scripture to which the revisionist of whom we are speaking appeals; that is, Scripture apart from any and all interpretation of it. When, therefore, the advocate of revision demands that the Westminster Confession be 'conformed to Scripture', he means conformation to Scripture as he and those like him read and explain it. It is impossible to make abstract Scripture the rule of faith for either an individual or a denomination. No Christian body has ever subscribed to the Bible merely as a printed book. A person who should write his name on the blank leaf of the Bible and say that his doctrinal belief was between the covers, would convey no definite information as to his creed. He might be a Socinian, or a Calvinist, or anywhere between these extremes. The only question, consequently, before the Presbyterian Church is, Whether the Confession shall be kept conformed to Scripture as the Calvinist understands it, or as the non-Calvinist or anti-Calvinist understands it; whether it shall continue to present that interpretation of Scripture which goes under the names of Augustine and Calvin, of Heidelberg, Dort, and Westminster, or that which goes under some other name, say that of 'modern exegesis', or of 'progressive theology'. The Presbyterian Church has decided in favor of the first proposition.

The question, What is Calvinism? is mainly one of reasoning and discrimination. It relates to a matter of fact. This question will answer itself in the discussion now going on; for this theological system possesses as distinctive features as the Copernican astronomy, and it will be as impossible to confuse and unsettle the religious world respecting the former, as it would be to confuse and unsettle the scientific world respecting the latter. The essential parts of this system are the well-known five points of Calvinism, namely, total depravity in distinction from partial; unconditional election in distinction from conditional; irresistible regenerating grace in distinction from resistible; limited redemption (not atonement) in distinction from universal; the certain perseverance of the regenerate in distinction from their possible apostasy. No one of these points can be rejected without impairing the integrity of Calvinism, any more than one of the points of the mariners' compass can be omitted and the scheme be complete; any more than one of the contrary five points of Arminianism can be deleted and the theory remain unaltered.

The 'Institutes' of Calvin, after all the development of

the Reformed or Calvinistic type of doctrine by later theologians, still remains one of the best statements of this powerful system. The keen and aquiline eye of the most scientific theologian of the Reformation saw the fundamental truths of revelation with an accuracy and precision that required no correction on his part. The great work of his early manhood remained essentially unchanged by him to the end of his career, and since his day it has laid at the foundation of all subsequent theologizing of this class, as the *Principia* of Newton has under all the succeeding mathematics of Europe. While, however, a revision of the Westminster Standards that shall be true to their structure and system does not require that the peculiarities of individual Calvinists, even of Calvin himself, or of Calvinistic schools should be followed, it does require that all of those constituent and formative tenets by which Augustinianism differs from Semi-Pelagianism, and Calvinism from Arminianism, shall be reaffirmed and maintained. The revision must be conformed to the historical Calvinism as stated in the principal Reformed or Calvinistic *creeds*, and not to Calvinism as constructed by any particular *theologian*, however able or popular in his own day and denomination.

The Christian religion contains certain truths that are so indisputably taught in the Christian Scriptures, that their acceptance is necessary in order to be a Christian in the sense in which the first disciples were so called at Antioch. They are the doctrines of the Trinity and incarnation, of apostasy and redemption, as they are generally and largely enunciated in the Apostles' and Nicene creeds. Respecting these, there has been little disagreement in ancient, mediæval, and modern Christendom. The Christian religion also contains certain other truths which, both in the Scriptures and in the doctrinal systems constructed out of them, are implications and deductions from these cardinal doctrines. It is in reference to this class of more strict and precise tenets, that evangelical Christendom has from the first been divided into two great divisons. In respect to them, the ancient theologian was either Augustinian or Semi-Pelagian; the modern theologian is either Calvinistic or Arminian. The difference between them relates principally to the more exact definition of original sin, of human freedom and ability, and of the Divine sovereignty and decrees. So long as Christian believers see through a glass darkly, there will be a speculative difference between them on these abstruser parts of revelation that will affect more or less the style of the religious experience, and make separate religious organizations desirable. This difference has for fifteen centuries crystallized into two sharply-edged types of theology, and there are no signs that one will outreason and conquer the other. Calvinism and Calvinistic denominations will probably continue to exist to the end of time; and so will Arminianism and Arminian denominations. In the future, as in the past, all evangelical believers will belong either to one dogmatic division or the other. It is better, in these circumstances, that both shall live and work side by side in frank and respectful recognition of each other, than to destroy the self-consistence of each by an attempt to combine both in a single system. Only these two general schemes of Christian doctrine are logically possible; for schemes that deny the Trinity and incarnation, the apostasy and redemption, are Deistic, not Christian. Both scientific theology and dogmatic history evince that there is no *tertium quid* between Calvinism and Arminianism, and that the choice of an individual or a denomination, consequently, lies between one or the other. Semi-Pelagianism was a real mid-point between the tenets of Augustine and those of Pelagius; but there is no true intermediate between the

[149]

system of Calvin and that of Arminius. In the history of doctrine there are sometimes semi-quavers, but demi-semi-quavers never.

Such being the facts, it is of the utmost importance to the Presbyterian Church that it retain the historical Calvinism upon which it was founded, and by which it has prospered. But it is of even greater importance to the whole world. It is a common remark of historians and philosophers, that Calvinism lays very deep the foundations of religious belief, of moral order, of civil society, and general intelligence and virtue, and that forms of government and social institutions which rest upon it are invincible, and 'cannot but by annihilating die'. Should this type of doctrine and this form of the religious experience disappear, Christendom would lose its balance-wheel. For it is no disparagement of the energy of evangelical Protestantism of all varieties, in the defence of the common faith, and the war upon the common unbelief, to say that the Genevan theology is always in the front whenever a fearless position has to be taken in behalf of an unpopular but revealed truth; whenever the Christian herald must announce the solemn alternatives of salvation and perdition to a sensuous, a pleasure-loving, and an irritable generation; whenever, in short, the stern and severe work of the perpetual campaign on earth against moral evil has to be done. The best interests of the Christian religion and Church require the continual existence and influence of that comprehensive and self-consistent creed which Augustine formulated out of Scripture, and Calvin reaffirmed and re-enforced. Evangelical Arminians who do not adopt it feel its influence, praying it in their prayers and singing it in their hymns; and Rationalists of all grades while recoiling from it acknowledge its massiveness and strength. It may, therefore, be confidently expected that whatever be the fortunes of a particular Church, or the tendencies of a particular time, this form of doctrine will perpetually survive in Christendom like the Scriptures out of which it was derived.

15: *Denominational Honesty and Honor*

Honesty is as important in theology as in trade and commerce, in a religious denomination as in a political party. Denominational honesty consists, first, in a clear unambiguous statement by a Church of its doctrinal belief; and, second, in an unequivocal and sincere adoption of it by its members. Both are requisite. If a particular denomination makes a loose statement of its belief which is capable of being construed in more than one sense, it is so far dishonest. If the creed of the denomination is well-drawn and plain, but the membership subscribe to it with mental reservation and insincerity, the denomination is dishonest. Honesty and sincerity are founded in clear conviction, and clear conviction is founded in the knowledge and acknowledgment of the truth. Heresy is a sin, and is classed by St. Paul among the 'works of the flesh', along with 'adultery, idolatry, murder, envy, and hatred', which exclude from the kingdom of God (*Gal. 5: 19–21*). But heresy is not so great a sin as dishonesty. There may be honest heresy, but not honest dishonesty. A heretic who acknowledges that he is such, is a better man than he who pretends to be orthodox while subscribing to a creed which he dislikes, and which he saps under pretence of improving it and adapting it to the times. The honest heretic leaves the Church with which he no longer agrees; but the insincere subscriber remains within it in order to carry out his plan of demoralization.

The recent discussions in the Presbyterian Church have

disclosed a difference of sentiment respecting the value of denominational honesty. Some of the secular newspapers charge intolerance and persecution upon Presbyterians, when departures from the church creed are made the subject of judicial inquiry, and when individuals are required to conform their teaching from the pulpit or the chair to the denominational standards. In this way a part of the public press is conniving at denominational dishonesty. It would permit church officers to subscribe to a creed and derive the benefit of subscription in the form of reputation or emolument, while working against it. The creed of a Church is a solemn *contract* between church-members; even more so than the platform of a political party is between politicans. The immorality of violating a contract, a portion of the press does not seem to perceive when a religious denomination is concerned; but when a political party is the body to be affected by the breach of a pledge, none are sharper to see and none are more vehement to denounce the double-dealing. Should a faction arise within the Republican party, for example, and endeavor to alter the platform while still retaining the offices and salaries which they had secured by professing entire allegiance to the party, and promising to adopt the fundamental principles upon which it was founded and by which it is distinguished from the Democratic and other political parties, the charge of political dishonesty would ring through the whole rank and file of Republicanism. And when in the exercise of party discipline such factionists are turned out of office, and perhaps expelled from the political organization, if the cry of political heresy-hunting and persecution should be raised, the only answer vouchsafed by the Republican press would be that of scorn. When political dishonesty would claim toleration under cover of more 'liberal' politics than the party is favoring, and would keep hold on party emoluments while advocating different sentiments from those of the mass of the party, it is curtly told that no one is compelled to join the Republican party or to remain in it, but that if a person does join it or remain in it, he must strictly adopt the party creed and make no attempts, secret or open, to alter it. That a Republican creed is for Republicans and no others, seems to be agreed on all sides; but that a Calvinistic creed is for Calvinists and no others, seems to be doubted by some.

The advocates of this view of a church creed and of creed subscription defend it upon the ground that it is proper to introduce improvements into a denominational creed; that the progress in physics and the spirit of the age require new statements of ethics and religion; and that this justifies the rise within a denomination of a party to make them, and requires that the denomination quietly look on and see it done. This means, for illustration, that a Church adopting the historical eschatology is bound to allow such of its members as think restorationism is an improvement, to attempt the introduction of it into the articles of faith; or that a Church adopting the Wesleyan Arminianism is obligated to let any of its members who think uncondi- tional election preferable to conditional, endeavor to Calvinize it by introducing this tenet. But should a corresponding liberty be demanded in the political sphere, it would meet with no favor. If in the heart of the Democratic party a school should arise who should claim the right, while still remaining in the party, to convert the body to Republican principles and measures, it would be told that the proper place for such a project is outside of Democracy, not within it. The right of the school to its own opinions would not be disputed, but the right to maintain and spread them with the funds and influence of the Democratic party would be denied. Democrats to a man would employ Luther's illustration in a similar instance: 'We cannot prevent the birds from flying over our heads, but we can prevent them from making their nests in our hair'. They would say to the malcontents, 'We cannot prevent you from having your own peculiar views and do not desire to, but you have no right to ventilate them in our organization'. Should the officers of the New York custom-house or post-office insist upon employing the salaries of these large institutions in transforming the politics of the party that placed them there, no cry of 'persecution' would deter the party from immediately cashiering the whole set. And yet some of the secular press, and some also of the religious, contend that it is proper for subscribers to the Westminster Confession to attempt a radical alteration of the denominational theology from within the denomination, and that it is suppressing free inquiry and the right of private judgment when seven-eighths of the Presbyterian Church represented in its highest court, put a veto upon such an attempt.

In such ecclesiastical action there is no denial of the right of private judgment, and of free inquiry into any system of doctrine whatever; only, it is claimed that those who dissent from the accepted creed of the denomination, if they are a minority, must go outside of it if they wish to construct a new scheme. The satisfied majority have the right of free inquiry and private judgment as well as the dissatisfied minority, and in the exercise of it stand by the creed as it is. Consequently, if discontent with the denominational standard arises in the minds of some, the proper place for their experiments in theologizing is within a new organization, and not in the old one which does not like their experiments. For this reason, from time immemorial, a religious denomination has always claimed the right to expel persons who are heretics as judged by the denominational creed. Only in this way can a denomination live and prosper. To throw down its doctrinal limits and convert itself into an unfenced common for all varieties of belief to ramble over, would not be useful either to society or religion.

But here the question arises, Who is to interpret the church creed, and say whether a proposed scheme of doctrine agrees with it, or contradicts it? Who is to say what is heresy from the stand-point of the denominational system? Certainly the denomination, and not the individual or school which is charged with heresy. This is a point of great importance. For those who are charged with heterodoxy commonly define orthodoxy in their own way, and claim not to have departed from what they regard as the essentials of the denominational system. The Arminian party in the Dort controversy contended that their modifications of doctrine were moderate and not antagonistic to the Reformed creeds. The Semi-Arians in the English Church asserted that their view of the Trinity did not differ essentially from that of the Nicene fathers. In each of these instances, the accused party complained that their statements were misapprehended by their opponents, and contended that the Church was mistaken in supposing that they could not be harmonized with the ancestral faith. The same assertion of being misunderstood and the same claim to be orthodox, marks the existing trial in the Presbyterian Church.

Now in determining what is the true meaning of the phraseology in a proposed alteration of the denominational creed, and what will be the natural influence of it if it is allowed to be taught, it is plain that it is for the denomination to decide. In case of a difference in understanding and interpreting a written document containing proposed changes in the church creed, the rule of the common law applies, that the accused party cannot be the final judge of the meaning and tendency of his own document, but that the court must be. And the denomination is the court. There is no hardship or unfairness in this. A denominational judgment is very certain to be equitable, be it in Church or State. The history of politics shows that the decisions of the great political parties respecting the real meaning of their platforms, and the conformity of individuals with them, have generally been correct. And the history of religion also shows that the judgments of the great ecclesiastical bodies respecting the teachings of their standards, and the agreement or disagreement of particular schools of theology with them, have been accurate. Those individuals and parties who have been declared to be heterodox, politically or theologically, by the deliberate vote of the body to which they belonged, have generally been so. It is rare that the majority has been in error, and the minority in the right.

Denominational honesty is closely connected with denominational honor. Those churches which have been the most frank in announcing their creed, and the most strict in insisting upon an honest interpretation and adoption of it by their membership, have been characterized by a scrupulous regard for the rights of other churches. Being satisfied with their own doctrinal position, and confident of the truth of their articles of faith, they have not invaded other denominations in order to alter their creed or to obtain their prestige. In this respect, the Calvinists of Christendom compare favorably with some of their opponents who charge them with illiberality and bigotry. It is true that in the times when the union of Church and State was universal, and the spread of any other religion but that of the State was regarded as menacing to the political weal, Calvinists like all other religious parties endeavored to suppress all creeds but the established. But they were ever in the van for the separation of Church and State, and for the religious toleration which naturally accompanies this. And ever since religious toleration has become the principle of Christendom, and the Protestant right of private judgment has become dominant, Calvinism has not been intolerant, or disposed to interfere with the creeds, institutions, and emoluments of other churches. It sets a good example in this respect. There is no instance upon record, that we remember, in which Calvinists have secretly tampered with the creed of another ecclesiastical body, and endeavored to seduce its membership from their loyalty to the articles of belief publicly adopted by them. From their own open and declared Calvinistic position, they have of course criticized and opposed other creeds, because they believed them to be more or less erroneous, but they have never adopted the plan of creeping into another denomination by subscribing to its articles, and then from that position endeavoring to revolutionize the body which it professed to join in good faith. No part of Christendom has been more free from insincerity and dissimulation than the Calvinistic churches.

Appendix: *The Significance of the Westminster Standards as a Creed*[*]

The significance of the Westminster Standards as a creed is to be found in the three facts that, historically speaking, they are the final crystallization of the elements of evangelical religion, after the conflicts of sixteen hundred years; scientifically speaking, they are the richest and most precise and best guarded statement ever penned of all that enters into evangelical religion and of all that must be safeguarded if evangelical religion is to persist in the world; and, religiously speaking, they are a notable monument of spiritual religion.

1. The gospel of the grace of God, or evangelical religion as we call it today, is, of course, the whole burden of the Scriptural revelation. But the Scriptural revelation does not supply the starting point, but the goal of the development of doctrine in the Church. There is a great gulf cleft between the writings of the apostles and their immediate successors, which is in nothing more marked than just in the slight grasp which the latter have on the principles of evangelical religion. It was not until Augustine, in opposition to the audacious assaults of Pelagianism, recovered for it the treasures of the gospel of grace, that the Church grasped them with any fulness or firmness. Nor even then was it able to retain them in their

*This is a summary of an address 'delivered, on its appointment, before the Presbytery of New York, Nov. 8, 1897' and reprinted in *Selected Shorter Writings of Benjamin B. Warfield*, ed. J. E. Meeter, vol. 2.

purity. The light which Augustine kindled faded again steadily until it was rekindled by the Reformation. It was once more obscured for the Lutheran churches by Melanchthonian synergism and the subsequent developments. Only among the Reformed was it retained in all its brightness, and that not without a struggle against not merely external foes but internal treason. In these struggles, however, the gem of the gospel was cut and polished, and it is on this account that the enunciation of the gospel in the Reformed Confessions attains its highest purity, and that among other Reformed Confessions the Westminster Confession, the product of the Puritan conflict, reaches a perfection of statement never elsewhere achieved.

2. It is incident to this, its historical origin, that the statement given of the gospel in the Westminster Standards touches the high-water mark of the scientific statement of the elements of evangelical religion. For, a higher scientific quality of doctrinal statement is attainable through the vital processes of controversy than through the cool efforts of closet construction. The scientific character of the Nicene and Chalcedonian definitions are due to this cause; and the Westminster Standards are the products of a similar history, and can lay claim to like finality in their sphere. The perennial foes of evengelical religion – sacerdotalism and humanitarianism – received not only their most powerful embodiment but also their most insidious and subtle manifestations in the age in which the Westminster theology was being prepared; and, in conflict with them, the most perfect statement of evangelical religion was necessarily wrought out. As truly as in the cases of the Nicene and Chalcedonian formularies, the Westminster Standards mark an epoch in the history of human reflection on the truths of the gospel – an epoch in the attainment and registry of doctrinal truth;

and as truly in the one case as in the other the statements they give of the truths that fall in their sphere are scientifically final. All attempts at restatement must either repeat their definitions or fall away from the purity of their conceptions or the justness of their language.

3. A scientific statement of vital truth, originating in organic controversy, cannot possibly lack in spiritual quality. It is the product of intellect working only under the impulse of the heart, and must be a monument of the religious life. This is true of all the great credal statements, and pre-eminently true of the Westminster Standards. Their authors were men of learning and philosophic grasp; but above all of piety. Their interest was not in speculative construction, but in the protection of their flocks from deadly error. It results from the very nature of the case, therefore, that it is a religious document which they have given us; and the nicety of its balance in conceiving and the precision of its language in stating truth, will seem to us scholastic only in proportion as our religious life is less developed than theirs. It requires a well-closed vessel to keep out all corrupting germs; and it requires a wide experience and a nice appreciation of what true holiness is to estimate at their true value the expedients used for the exclusion of the corrupting germs. In proportion as our own religious life flows in a deep and broad stream, in that proportion will we find spiritual delight in the Westminster Standards.

Surely blessed are the churches which feed upon such meat! May God Almighty infuse their strength into our bones, and their beauty into our flesh, and enable us to justify our inheritance by unfolding into life, in all its completeness and richness, the precious gospel which they have enfolded for us in their protecting envelope of sound words!